SCHOLASTIC'S
A+ GUIDE TO
GRAMMAR

Over a million junior high and high school students have used Scholastic's A+ Guides to raise their grades, do better in every subject, and *enjoy* school more. Now you can, too!

SCHOLASTIC'S A+
GUIDE TO GOOD GRADES

SCHOLASTIC'S A+
GUIDE TO GOOD WRITING

SCHOLASTIC'S A+
GUIDE TO TAKING TESTS

SCHOLASTIC'S A+
GUIDE TO GRAMMAR

SCHOLASTIC'S A+
GUIDE TO RESEARCH AND TERM PAPERS

SCHOLASTIC'S A+
GUIDE TO BOOK REPORTS

SCHOLASTIC'S A+ GUIDE TO GRAMMAR

VICKI TYLER

SCHOLASTIC INC.
New York Toronto London Auckland Sydney

ISBN 0-590-33316-X

Copyright © 1981 by Vicki Tyler. All rights reserved. Published by Scholastic Inc.

12 11 10 9 8 7 6 5 4 3 2   7 8/8

Printed in the U.S.A.   01

FIND IT FAST!

This handbook contains everything you need to know about grammar.

Below is a list of the grammar tips you might need to look up in a hurry. The following chart tells you on what pages you can find information on specific topics.

HERE'S WHERE TO FIND OUT

HERE'S WHERE TO LOOK UP CONFUSING WORDS AND PHRASES

TABLE OF CONTENTS

Chapter 1

GRAMMAR
Who Needs It?

Believe it or not, you were a whiz at grammar before you even learned to read or write. By the time you were six years old, you already had the basics figured out. You already knew how to combine subjects, verbs, modifiers, and complements (you didn't call them that, of course) into good English sentences—groups of words that made sense.

Unfortunately, the kind of expertise you had when you were six won't help you fix a confusing sentence in your composition, or study for an important English exam, or use words correctly when you want to make a good impression. To make sure your English is working *for* you instead of *against* you, it's a good idea to become familiar with the rules of Standard English. Standard English is the language that most educated speakers and writers try to use. Its rules are followed in most offices, colleges, books, newspapers, magazines, and television programs. You've probably studied these rules in English class for years, but—as you know—it's sometimes hard to remember the right rules at the right time. What you need is practice—and a good handbook to help you out when you get stuck.

This book is your own portable, pocket-sized

grammar survival kit. It's a step-by-step rundown of all those hard-to-remember terms and rules (just in case you want to sit down and read it all the way through!). But it's also designed so that you can dip in and find what you want in a hurry. In the back of the book there's a "Use It Right" glossary that explains all those confusing words that are so easy to get mixed up. There are also handy "Capitalization Pointers" and "Punctuation Pointers" at the back of the book. In the front of the book there's a "Find It Fast" chart, which tells you where to look to find the grammar tips you're most likely to want to know . . . *fast*! And there are dozens of other charts throughout the book to help you learn grammar at a glance.

Parting Words: For those of you who think that studying grammar is like going to the dentist, here is *The A+ Guide to Grammar*'s guarantee: It won't hurt as much as you think; it definitely helps; and you *will* survive!

SOMETIMES IT MAKES A DIFFERENCE!

Some rules of grammar and usage are based strictly on custom: An "incorrect" usage sometimes expressess a thought just as clearly as "correct" usage. But sometimes using a little bit of grammar can make a big difference and avoid a great deal of confusion, as the sentences below demonstrate:

1. *After my brother gave the dog a bath, he shook out his fur and barked.*

Who barked—the brother or the dog? To avoid confusing (and sometimes hilarious) bloopers like this, see "Beware of the Slippery Pronoun," p. 48.

2. *While running down the street, my homework blew out of my notebook.*

Unless your homework wears jogging shoes, your English teacher will never fall for this excuse. To find out how to revise it, see "Danger: Dangling Modifiers," p. 120 (Your English teacher probably still won't believe your excuse, but he or she might give you some points for expressing it grammatically!)

3. *My boyfriend likes pizza more than me.*

Any girl who believes this had better find another boyfriend—or look up "How to Choose the Right Pronoun," pp. 30–33.

Chapter 2

DEFINE YOUR TERMS

THE PARTS OF SPEECH

The *parts of speech* are the eight categories that describe how words can be used in a sentence. They are: *noun, pronoun, verb, adjective, adverb, preposition, conjunction,* and *interjection*.

PART OF SPEECH	DEFINITION	EXAMPLES
noun	names a person, place, thing, idea, or quality	teenager, Kate, town, freedom, Hollywood, hamburger, music, beauty
pronoun	takes the place of a noun	we, her, ours, it, everybody, who
verb	expresses action, being, or state of being	tackles, drove, is, has grown, think, become
adjective	tells more about a noun or pronoun	hilarious, soft, two, incredible, young, fearless

adverb	tells more about a verb, adjective, or another adverb	softly, fearlessly, yesterday, very, twice
preposition	relates a noun or pronoun to another word in a sentence	*into the gym, with love, except for me
conjunction	connects words or groups of words	and, but, or, because, if
interjection	expresses strong feeling	Ouch! Wow! Oh, no!

*Each example is a *prepositional phrase*. The italicized word in each example is the *preposition*.

MORE ABOUT PARTS OF SPEECH

Here are some clues that can help you decide what part of speech a word is. They won't always work for every word, but the clues will give you a better idea of how parts of speech work. REMEMBER: Sometimes the same word can fit the requirements for several different parts of speech. The final test is always *how the word is used in a sentence*.

IT'S PROBABLY A *NOUN* IF. . .

*It makes sense in one or both of the blanks below:
(The) _____ is/are interesting.
Do you like (the) _____?

5

EXAMPLES:

The *shows* are interesting.

Do you like the *singer*?

Tennis is interesting.

Do you like *responsibility*?

* It has a *plural* form (a form that means more than one).

EXAMPLES:

boy-*boys*   mystery-*mysteries*
woman-*women*

* It has a *possessive* form (a form that shows that something belongs to the noun).

EXAMPLES:

the *singer's* voice

the *car's* transmission

Centerville's only skating rink

Fleetwood Mac's drummer

* It can follow the word *the* and other "noun markers" such as *a, an, that, these, those, her, their, many,* etc.

EXAMPLES:

the *singer*, those *boys*, her *voice*

EXTRA CLUE: The following words are all nouns and show some common noun endings: happi*ness*, concentra*tion*, govern*ment*, pharma*cist*, eleg*ance*, hero*ism*, employ*ee*, responsibil*ity*, pati*ence*, consist*ency*.

SEE CHAPTER 3 FOR MORE INFORMATION.

IT'S PROBABLY A *PRONOUN* IF. . .

It makes sense in the same parts of the sentence that a noun does, BUT you CANNOT put *the* in front of it.

EXAMPLES:

It is interesting.   Do you like *them*?

They are interesting.

NOTE: Many pronouns do not fit this description.

EXAMPLES:

our, which, themselves

SEE CHAPTER 4 FOR MORE INFORMATION.

IT'S PROBABLY A *VERB* IF. . .

* It makes sense in the blanks below.

  Let's _____.   I can _____ (it).

  EXAMPLES:

  Let's *try*.   I can *go*.   I can *start* it.

* You can put an auxiliary (helping verb) in front of it.

  EXAMPLES:

  They *have tried*.   I *might go*.

  She *will start* it.

* You can add *-ed* or *-d* at the end of it to indicate time in the past.

  NOTE: There are many exceptions to this rule.

SEE CHAPTER 5 FOR MORE INFORMATION.

IT'S PROBABLY AN *ADJECTIVE* IF. . .

* It tells *how many*, *what kind*, or *which one*.
* It makes sense in one or all of the blanks below.

We saw _____ thing(s).   He was very
_____.   It was very _____.

EXAMPLES:

We saw *beautiful* things. He was very *tall*.
     three   It was very
     many   *ridiculous*.
     the last
     terrible

EXTRA CLUE: The following words are all adjectives and show some common adjective endings: ador*able*, ordin*ary*, terrif*ic*, beauti*ful*, gener*ous*.

SEE CHAPTER 6 FOR MORE INFORMATION.

IT'S PROBABLY AN *ADVERB* IF. . .

* It tells *where*, *when*, *how*, *how many times*, *in what order*, or *to what degree*.

* It makes sense in the blank below.
He did it _____.

EXAMPLES:

He did it *there*.
       well.
       yesterday.
       first.
       twice.

SEE CHAPTER 6 FOR MORE INFORMATION.

IT'S PROBABLY A *PREPOSITION* IF...

* It makes sense in the blank below:

  It went _____ the thing.

  NOTE: This test does not work for the most common preposition: *of*.

* It shows the relationship between the noun or pronoun that comes after it and some other word in the sentence. NOTE: If no noun or pronoun comes after it, it is not a preposition.

  EXAMPLES:

  The game is *over*. (*Over* is an adjective modifying *game*.)

  She came *over*. (*Over* is an adverb modifying *came*.)

  We flew *over* the city. (*Over* is a preposition that shows the relationship between *flew* and *city*.)

TIME OUT: Getting Down to the Nitty Gritty

The word *down* is used in five different ways in the following sentences. Can you tell what part of speech it is in each sentence? (The answers are printed upside "down" on p. 10.)

1. Our team made a first *down* on the ten-yard line.
2. Hank can *down* a milkshake in thirty seconds flat.
3. My sister bought a *down* jacket.
4. What goes up must come *down*.
5. Janet screamed as the roller coaster went *down* the hill.

9

THE PARTS OF THE SENTENCE

A *sentence* is a word or group of words that expresses a complete thought. A sentence makes sense and sounds complete standing alone.

EXAMPLES:

Today is my birthday.   Have you seen Terry?

She likes ice cream.   The bell rang.

* A sentence should begin with a *capital letter* and end with a *period, question mark,* or *exclamation mark*.

* A sentence has two main parts: a *subject* and a *predicate*.

SUBJECTS AND PREDICATES

* The *subject* tells *who* or *what* the sentence is about. It names the person or thing being talked about. The *predicate* tells what is being said about the subject. It often tells what the subject *does* or *did*— or what the subject *is* or *was*.

EXAMPLES:

Subjects	Predicates
The tall *boy* in the green sweater	*asked* Sally her name in study hall last period.
Our last *chance* to get into the finals	*was* last Saturday night at ten-thirty.

ANSWERS: 1. noun, 2. verb, 3. adjective, 4. adverb, 5. preposition.

10

Complete Subject and Complete Predicate

The subjects shown above are *complete subjects*. Each includes a key *noun* or *pronoun* plus words that describe the noun or pronoun. The predicates shown above are *complete predicates*. Each includes a *verb* plus words that add to or complete the meaning of the verb.

Simple Subject and Simple Predicate

The simple subject and the simple predicate are the key words of the sentence. The *simple subject* is the key noun or pronoun that tells who or what the sentence is about. The *simple predicate* is the verb by itself. In the examples above, the simple subjects and simple predicates are the words in *italics*.

NOTE: Sometimes the verb consists of more than one word.

EXAMPLE:

<u>I</u> / have been <u>going</u> there for three years.

NOTE: Sometimes, in a short sentence, the simple subject is the complete subject and the verb is the complete predicate.

EXAMPLES:

<u>I</u> / am <u>going</u>.   Jack <u>Smith</u> / <u>left</u>.   <u>Who</u> / <u>cares</u>?

HOW TO FIND SIMPLE SUBJECTS AND VERBS

* Find the verb first.

  Find the verb first—the word or words that express the action or state of being. Then find the subject by asking *who* or *what* does the action or being.

11

EXAMPLE:

The magician's assistant suddenly vanished.

What word expresses the action? *Vanished* is the verb.

Who vanished? *Assistant* is the subject.

* Questions

In most sentences, the subject comes before the verb. But in some sentences all or part of the verb comes first. This happens most often in questions. To find the subject in a question, *first change the question to a statement*. The subject and the verb will be easier to find.

EXAMPLE:

Question: Why did you call me?

Change to statement: You did call me.

* Here/there

The words *here* and *there* are NEVER subjects, even when they come at the beginning of the sentence.

EXAMPLES:

Here is your blue sweater.

There he is.

* Never look in prepositional phrases.

Never look for the simple subject in a prepositional phrase. Prepositional phrases are always modifiers.

EXAMPLES:

One of the buttons / is coming loose.

A pint of raspberries / doesn't last long.

12

> * "You" understood
>
> In a sentence that makes a command or request, there appears to be no subject. We say that the subject *you* is understood.
>
> EXAMPLES:
>
> (Y͜ou) C͟ome here!
>
> (Y͜ou) M͟eet me at eight.

Compound Subjects and Compound Verbs

* Some sentences have a *compound subject*. This means that two or more subjects joined by *and* or *or* have the same verb.

EXAMPLES:

S͟ue, G͟ail, and P͟am / are c͟oming to my party.

Either the q͟uarterback or the e͟nd / will r͟eceive the award.

* Some sentences have a *compound verb* (also called a *compound predicate*). This means that two or more verbs joined by *and* or *or* have the same subject.

EXAMPLES:

W͟e / w͟ent downtown and a͟te in a fancy restaurant.

J͟ohn / d͟evoured all the cake, d͟rank all the milk, and a͟sked for more.

* Some sentences have *both* a compound subject and a compound verb. This means that two or more subjects share two or more verbs.

EXAMPLES:

My s͟isters and I͟ / are t͟raveling together and s͟haring expenses.

Either <u>Jack</u>^s or his <u>friend</u>^s / <u>will replace</u>^v the fan belt and <u>tune</u>^v the engine.

NOTE: Sentences that have compound subjects and compound predicates are not necessarily compound sentences. This term has a special meaning. See p. 127.

COMPLEMENTS

Often a subject and a verb will need another word or words to complete the thought of the sentence. For example, look at these subject-verb combinations: *he kicked, she handed, I am, Sue is, we named.* In each case, there seems to be something missing. What these sentences need are special completers called *complements*. There are five different kinds of complements:

* The *direct object* (D.O.) is a noun or pronoun that tells *who* or *what* receives the action of the verb. That is, it tells *who* or *what* was kicked, sent, named, etc.

EXAMPLE:
He kicked the *ball*^{D.O.} through the goalposts.

* The *indirect object* (I.O.) is a noun or pronoun that tells *to whom, to what, for whom,* or *for what* an action is done.

EXAMPLES:
She handed *me*^{I.O.} the *note*^{D.O.}.
They gave *her*^{I.O.} a surprise *party*^{D.O.}.
She gave the *dog*^{I.O.} a *bone*^{D.O.}.

* The *predicate nominative* (P.N.) is a noun or pronoun that comes after the verb and identifies the subject.

14

EXAMPLES:
I am the *champion*.^{P.N.}
Bonnie is my *sister*.^{P.N.}

*The *predicate adjective* (P.A.) is an adjective that comes after the verb and describes the subject.

EXAMPLE:
Sue is *excited* about going to the game.^{P.A.}

*The *object complement* (O.C.) is a noun or adjective that follows the direct object and refers to it.

EXAMPLES:
We named our *cat* *Popeye*.^{D.O. O.C.}
I hold *you* *responsible*.^{D.O. O.C.}

DIRECT OR INDIRECT OBJECT?

* An *indirect* object can appear only in combination with a direct object. It never appears alone. When an action verb is followed by just one noun or pronoun, that noun or pronoun is probably a direct object.

EXAMPLE:
I sent a *letter*.^{D.O.}

* When an action verb has two complements, *find the direct object first* by asking *who* or *what* receives the action. Then, see if there is a word that tells *to whom*, *for whom*, *to what*, or *for what* an action is done. That word is the indirect object.

EXAMPLE:
I sent *Maureen* a *letter*.^{I.O. D.O.}

sent what? *Letter* is the direct object.

15

sent letter to whom? *Maureen* is the indirect object.

* The *indirect* object comes *between* the verb and the direct object. Here is the pattern for a sentence with an indirect object:

$$\underset{\text{S}}{\underline{\text{I}}} \quad \underset{\text{V}}{\underline{\text{made}}} \quad \underset{\text{I.O.}}{\text{Betty}} \quad \underset{\text{D.O.}}{\text{a } \textit{sandwich}}.$$

* If the words *to* or *for* actually appear before the noun, it cannot be an indrect object. When this happens, the noun is an object of the preposition.

EXAMPLES:

I gave Sandy a dollar.
(*Sandy* is the indirect object.)
I gave a dollar to Sandy.
(*Sandy* is the object of the preposition.)

EXTRA CLUE: The indirect object can usually be removed from the sentence, and the sentence will still make sense.

OTHER SENTENCE PARTS

* A *modifier* adds to or changes the meaning of another word. A modifier may be a single word or several words acting together. The most common modifiers include *adjectives*, *adverbs*, *prepositional phrases*, *participial phrases*, and *dependent clauses*.

* A *phrase* is a group of related words that does NOT have a subject and a predicate. Most phrases act as modifiers. (EXCEPTION: Verb phrases are never modifiers.)

* A *clause* is any group of words that has both a subject and a predicate. NOTE: Not all clauses are sentences.

An *independent* clause is one that can stand alone as a sentence. It makes sense and sounds complete by itself. A sentence consists of one or more independent clauses.

A *dependent* clause (also called a *subordinate* clause) is one that cannot stand alone. It is only part of a sentence and must be joined to an independent clause to make sense. There are three kinds of dependent clauses: *noun clauses, adjective clauses,* and *adverb clauses.*

END PUNCTUATION FOR SENTENCES

* A *declarative* sentence makes a statement.
  It ends with a period.

* An *interrogative* sentence asks a question.
  It ends with a question mark.

* An *imperative* sentence makes a request or gives an order.
  It ends with a period.

* An *exclamatory* sentence expresses strong feeling.
  It ends with an exclamation mark.

NOTE: Declarative, interrogative, and imperative sentences may all become exclamatory when expressed with strong feeling. In these cases, they may end with exclamation marks, BUT use exclamation marks sparingly, or they will lose their impact on your readers.

Chapter 3

WHAT'S IN A NAME?
All About Nouns

A *noun* names a person, place, thing, idea, or quality.

* A *proper noun* is the name of a *particular* person, place, or thing. Proper nouns begin with a capital letter.

EXAMPLES:

Melissa, Luke Skywalker, Ohio, Super Bowl

* A *common noun* does not tell the name of a particular person, place, or thing. It either refers to a whole category or to an individual that is not mentioned by name.

EXAMPLES:

girl, hero, state, game

NOTE: To make common nouns more specific, we add modifiers (the nouns are in italics): that *girl*, the *hero* of the movie, the *state* where I live, the most exciting football *game* of the year.

COMMON OR PROPER?
WHEN TO CAPITALIZE A NOUN

Turn to "Capitalization Pointers" on p. 150.

SPECIAL KINDS OF NOUNS

* An *abstract noun* names a quality or idea.

  EXAMPLES:

  Her *friendliness* surprised me.

  Honesty is important to me.

* A *collective noun* names a group or collection of persons or things.

  EXAMPLES:

  team, family, crowd, herd, audience

* A *compound noun* is made up of two or more words. Some compounds are written as separate words, some are hyphenated, and some are written as one word. Check your dictionary when you are not sure how to write a compound noun.

  EXAMPLES:

  newspaper, air conditioning, drive-in

NOUNS CAN BE SINGULAR OR PLURAL

Most nouns have a singular form and a plural form. A *singular* noun names only one person, place, or thing. A *plural* noun names more than one.

HOW TO MAKE NOUNS PLURAL

As you know, there are exceptions to every rule. Use your dictionary when you are not sure how to make a noun plural. If the plural is formed in a special way, it will usually be listed right at the beginning of the dictionary entry, before the definition.

* To make most nouns plural, just add *s* to the singular.

EXAMPLES:

pen-pens   apple-apples
television-televisions

* When the singular ends in *s*, *x*, *z*, *ch*, or *sh*, add *es*.

EXAMPLES:

glass-glasses   box-boxes
waltz-waltzes   crutch-crutches

* When the singular ends in *y*, follow these rules:
  * If a vowel comes right before the *y*, just add *s*:

  EXAMPLES:

  play-plays   monkey-monkeys

  * If a consonant comes right before the *y*, change the *y* to *i* and add *es*.

  EXAMPLES:

  army-armies   duty-duties

  * If the word is a proper noun, always just add *s*.

  EXAMPLES:

  The *Maloneys* and the *Haggertys* played bridge.

* When the singular ends in *f* or *fe*, it's a good idea to check your dictionary.

In some cases the plural is formed by just adding *s*.

EXAMPLES:

belief-beliefs   chief-chiefs

cliff-cliffs   safe-safes

In other cases, the plural is formed by changing the *f* or *fe* to *v* and adding *es*.

EXAMPLES:

wife-wives   half-halves   leaf-leaves

* When the singular ends in *o*, check your dictionary. In some cases, the plural is formed by adding *s*. In other cases, it is formed by adding *es*.

EXAMPLES:

piano-pianos   soprano-sopranos

potato-potatoes   hero-heroes

radio-radios

* A few plurals are formed in special ways. You just have to memorize them.

EXAMPLES:

child-children   mouse-mice

woman-women   foot-feet

* In a few cases, the plural is exactly the same as the singular.

EXAMPLES:

a new TV series-several new TV series

one deer-two deer   one sheep-two sheep

* When a compound noun is written as one word, add the plural suffix to the end of the entire word.

21

EXAMPLES:
hairdos, cupfuls

* When a compound noun is hyphenated or written as separate words, add the plural ending to the most important word, which is usually a noun.

EXAMPLES:
mother-in-law, mothers-in-law
(They are *mothers*, not *laws*.)
passer-by, passers-by
(They are *passers*, not *bys*.)
box office-box offices

EXCEPTIONS: foul-ups, drive-ins, sixteen-year-olds, etc.

* Some words borrowed from other languages keep their original plural forms.

EXAMPLES:

Singular	Plural
cri*sis*	cri*ses*
parenthe*sis*	parenthe*ses*
analy*sis*	analy*ses*
medi*um*	medi*a*
(TV is a medium.)	(TV, newspapers, and radio together are media.)

* Some nouns are always plural in form and use. They cannot be made singular, even when they mean one thing.

EXAMPLES:
My *jeans* are a little too short.
May I have those *scissors*?

22

* A few nouns look plural but are really singular.

EXAMPLES:

Measles is contagious.

The *news* is exciting.

Mathematics is her favorite subject.

* To form the plural of most proper nouns, just add *s*. If the proper noun ends in *s*, *x*, *z*, *ch*, or *sh*, add *es*.

EXAMPLES:

the Smiths, the Hanrattys, the Sanchezes, the Weisses, the D'Amatos, the Marches

NOUNS CAN SHOW POSSESSION

The *possessive* form of a noun shows ownership. If you get confused when you try to make a word possessive, you're not the only one. Even the experts disagree, sometimes. The chart below shows you a simple system to follow. The most important thing you have to decide is whether you are talking about one person or thing or more than one. That's where most people go wrong.

HOW TO MAKE NOUNS SHOW POSSESSION

* Singular Nouns

To make a *singular* noun possessive, add *'s*. Do this whether the noun already ends in *s* or not.

EXAMPLES:

Stephanie's   Charles's   Mrs. Jones's
the actress's part

* Plural Nouns

To make a plural noun possessive, follow these rules:

If the plural already ends in *s*, just add an apostrophe.

EXAMPLES:

There was a sale on *boys'* slacks.
(slacks for *boys*)

The *players'* uniforms were blue and gold.
(uniforms belonging to *players*)

If the plural does NOT end in *s*, add *'s*.

EXAMPLES:

Fran works at the *Children's* Hospital.
(hospital for *children*)

My mother belongs to the *women's* club in our town.
(club for *women*)

* Compound Nouns

To form the possessive of a compound noun, place the possessive ending after the *last* word.

EXAMPLES:

My mother-in-law's name is Mary.
(one mother-in-law, possession)

Our mothers-in-law met for the first time on Friday.
(more than one, no possession)

Our mothers-in-law's houses are very similar.
(more than one, possession)

NOTE: The last sentence above is correct, but it sounds awkward. You would probably be better off rewriting it as: *Our mothers-in-law have very similar houses.*

* Shared Ownership
  When two or more people possess the same thing, add the possessive ending only to the last-mentioned name.

  EXAMPLES:
  Bob and Nancy's engagement
  Cindy, Gail, and Susan's little brother

* Separate Ownership
  When two or more people possess things separately, add the possessive endings to *each noun*.

  EXAMPLES:
  Bob's and Nancy's horoscopes are very different.
  Cindy's, Gail's, and Susan's grades are better than mine.

* Using OF to Show Possession
  Another way to show ownership is to use a phrase beginning with *of*. This technique is usually used with objects that are not alive.

  EXAMPLE:
  the box's lid = the lid of the box

  NOTE: It's also a good idea to use an *of* phrase when an apostrophe might be confusing.

  EXAMPLE:
  the boy in the second row's shoes =
  the shoes of the boy in the second row

POSSESSIVE SOUND-ALIKES

One big problem with possessives is that different

forms of the noun often *sound* alike but are spelled differently. Again, the most important thing to do when you are trying to spell a possessive is to stop and think: Are you talking about one person or thing—or more than one? If you are talking about more than one, make sure the plural form is spelled correctly. Then follow the rules in the chart above.

EXAMPLES:

Most people would pronounce the italicized words in these sentences the same way. Yet, notice the differences in spelling and meaning. You can use these sentences as a guide to help you write possessives.

Mr. *Weiss's* new car had a flat tire.
(one person, possession)

All six of the *Weisses* had to walk home.
(more than one person, no possession)

The *Weisses'* house is always noisy.
(more than one, possession)

I stayed overnight at the *Weisses'*.
(more than one, possession; the word *house* is understood)

The *baby's* crying woke us up.
(one baby, possession)

The *babies* in the nursery were all asleep.
(more than one, no possession)

Babies' bones are not very strong.
(more than one, possession)

HELP WANTED: JOBS FOR NOUNS

What can nouns do in a sentence? Here is a brief rundown. (Each of these terms is explained in more detail in other parts of this book. Consult the index 26 to find out where.)

SUBJECT: tells who or what the sentence is about.

Tennis is my favorite sport.

DIRECT OBJECT: tells who or what receives the action of the verb.

Jack and I ate the whole *pie*.

INDIRECT OBJECT: tells to whom, for whom, to what, or for what an action is done.

She gave *Dave* your phone number.

PREDICATE NOUN: noun in the predicate that identifies the subject.

Sue is the best *skater* I know.

OBJECT COMPLEMENT: comes after the direct object and refers to it.

We elected her *president*.

APPOSITIVE: identifies the noun that comes right before it.

There's my friend *John*.

OBJECT OF THE PREPOSITION: is linked by the preposition to some other word in the sentence.

Let's get into the *car* and go!

NOUN OF DIRECT ADDRESS: names the person spoken to.

Jim, will you make up your mind?

MODIFIER: tells more about another noun.

She bought a beautiful *leather* coat.

NOTE: Any word, phrase, or clause that can do the same jobs that a noun does is called a *noun equivalent*. Some common noun equivalents are: *pronouns*, *gerunds*, *infinitives*, and *noun clauses*.

SEE: "Pronouns," Chapter 4
    "Gerunds," p. 95
    "Infinitives," p. 96
    "Noun Clauses," p. 141

Chapter 4

STAND-INS
All About Pronouns

A *pronoun* takes the place of a noun.

* There are six kinds of pronouns:

Personal: I, you, he, she, it, we, they, etc.
(see p. 28)

Interrogative: who? which? what?
(see p. 36)

Demonstrative: this, that, these, those
(see p. 39)

Indefinite: nothing, everybody, anyone, all, either, etc.
(see p. 41)

Reciprocal: each other, one another
(see p. 42)

Relative: who, which, that, etc.
(see p. 137)

PERSONAL PRONOUNS

Personal pronouns identify specific persons or things. They can refer to:

* the person(s) speaking
(called the *first person*): I, we

* The person(s) spoken to
  (called the *second person*): *you*

* the person(s) or thing(s) spoken about
  (called the *third person*): *he, she, it, they*

EXAMPLES:
1st   2nd 3rd
I told *you he* would be here.
3rd   1st   2nd
He asked *me* to help *you*.

Personal pronouns can be singular or plural.

EXAMPLES:

singular = one person or thing: I, you, he, she, it

plural = more than one: we, you, they

PRONOUN CASES

Because pronouns take the place of nouns, they can do the same jobs that nouns do in a sentence. They can be subjects, direct objects, indirect objects, objects of the preposition, predicate pronouns (predicate nominatives), and appositives. (These terms are defined in Chapter 3.)

* Different forms of a pronoun are used to do different jobs. These forms are called *cases*.

* Pronouns have three different cases: the *subjective* (sometimes called the nominative), the *objective* (sometimes called the accusative), and the *possessive*.

SUBJECTIVE CASE PRONOUNS:

Used as subjects and predicate pronouns

PERSON	SINGULAR	PLURAL
1st	I	we
2nd	you	you
3rd	he, she, it	they

29

OBJECTIVE CASE PRONOUNS:
Used as direct objects, indirect objects,
and objects of the preposition

PERSON	SINGULAR	PLURAL
1st	me	us
2nd	you	you
3rd	him, her, it	them

POSSESSIVE CASE PRONOUNS:
Used to show ownership

PERSON	SINGULAR	PLURAL
1st	my, mine	our, ours
2nd	your, yours	your, yours
3rd	his, her, hers, its	their, theirs

HOW TO CHOOSE THE RIGHT PRONOUN:
I/me, she/her, he/him, they/them

* Cross out extra subjects and objects.
When a pronoun is used by itself as a subject or object, most people will automatically choose the right form.

EXAMPLES:

(He)/Him helped me paint my room.

Why don't they ask she/(her) to help out?

Caroline wants to have lunch with I/(me).

BUT when there's more than one subject or object, it's easy to get confused.

EXAMPLES:

Rita and he/him helped me paint my room.

Why don't they ask Sylvia and she/her to help out?

Caroline wants to have lunch with you and I/me.

DON'T BE CONFUSED. JUST COVER UP THE EXTRA SUBJECT OR OBJECT AND READ THE SENTENCE WITH THE PRONOUN BY ITSELF AS THE SUBJECT OR OBJECT. YOU'LL ALMOST ALWAYS MAKE THE RIGHT CHOICE.

EXAMPLES:

~~Rita and~~ (he)/him helped me paint my room.

Why don't they ask ~~Sylvia and~~ she/(her) to help out?

Caroline wants to have lunch with ~~you and I~~/(me).

NOTE: When there are two pronouns in the subject or object, read each one separately to choose the right forms.

EXAMPLE:

She/Her and I/me take the same bus every morning.

(She)/Her takes the same bus every morning.

(I)/me take the same bus every morning.

She and I take the same bus every morning.

NOTE: Always say *between you and me,* NOT *between you and I.*

* Cross out other extra nouns.
  When a pronoun is followed by a noun, just cross out the noun and read the sentence without it. You'll probably choose the right pronoun.

EXAMPLES:

(We)/Us ~~boys~~ are all on the team.

Don't disturb we/(us) ~~mad scientists~~.

31

* Fill in the missing words.

There are two words missing at the end of the example below. Can you fill them in?

EXAMPLE:

I can run faster than he/him.

Give up? The missing words are *can run*. The sentence really means: *I can run faster than he/him can run*. After you fill in the missing words, it's easy to see that *he* is the right pronoun choice for this sentence.

Try this one:

EXAMPLE:

My boyfriend likes pizza more than I/me.

This sentence can go either way, depending on the missing words. Be careful to say what you mean!

My boyfriend likes pizza more than I/me (like pizza).

My boyfriend likes pizza more than (he likes) I/me.

NOW TRY THIS:

He calls me more often than she.

He calls me more often than her.

Which one means that he calls you more often than he calls her? Which one means that he calls you more often than she calls you?

* Use I, SHE, HE, and THEY after a BE verb. Even though this rule is not obeyed much in speaking (almost everyone says "It's me"), you should always obey it in your writing. Here's a clue to help you remember it: A sentence with a BE verb (am, is, are, was, has been, etc.) is usually reversible. That is,

The winner was she/her = She/Her was the winner.

When you reverse the sentence, it's easy to see that *she* is the right choice.

HOW TO CHOOSE THE RIGHT PRONOUN:
its/it's; your/you're; their/they're/there

A personal pronoun that shows possession NEVER takes an apostrophe. Any personal pronoun with an apostrophe is a *contraction* of two words.

* *its*: shows possession
  it's: contraction of *it is*

EXAMPLE:
It's time for someone to feed the cat and change *its* water.

* *your*: shows possession
  you're: contraction of *you are*

EXAMPLE:
You're saving *your* money for a stereo, aren't you?

* *their*: shows possession
  they're: contraction of *they are*
  there: adverb telling where

EXAMPLE:
They're hoping to go *there* on *their* vacation.

33

TWO KINDS OF POSSESSIVE PRONOUNS

* Some possessive pronouns always come before nouns and act as modifiers. For this reason, they are sometimes called *possessive adjectives*.

EXAMPLES:

my hat	*her* answer	*our* neighbors
your fault	*its* fur	*their* seats

* Other possessive pronouns, known as *absolute possessives*, never come before nouns. They stand alone and act just like nouns. They can be subjects, direct objects, objects of the preposition, etc.

EXAMPLES:

Mine was the last name to be called.

If you can't find an umbrella, Rose will lend you *hers*.

Mary's order finally appeared ten minutes after *ours*.

* The pronoun *his* can be either a possessive adjective or an absolute possessive.

EXAMPLES:

His answer is still "no."

Is your determination as strong as *his*?

COMPOUND PERSONAL PRONOUNS

The *compound personal pronouns* are:

PERSON	SINGULAR	PLURAL
1st	myself	ourselves
2nd	yourself	yourselves
3rd	himself, herself, itself	themselves

* A compound personal pronoun is sometimes used to give *emphasis* to a noun or another pronoun. It is then known as an *intensive pronoun*.

EXAMPLES:

I *myself* was not at the assembly when the principal cancelled the game.

Barbara *herself* said it wouldn't work!

* A compound personal pronoun may also be used as an object that refers back to the subject. It is then known as a *reflexive pronoun*.

EXAMPLES:

He disqualified *himself* from the race.

You should give *yourself* a chance to improve.

I'm always talking to *myself*.

USING COMPOUND PERSONAL PRONOUNS

* NEVER use *hisself* or *theirselves*. These are incorrect forms. Use *himself* and *themselves* instead.

* Don't use the word *myself* where *I* or *me* is correct.

Don't say:	Tim and myself were the first to arrive.
Say:	Tim and I were the first to arrive.
Don't say:	The sign was painted by Maria and myself.
Say:	The sign was painted by Maria and me.

INTERROGATIVE PRONOUNS

The pronouns *who*, *which*, and *what* are called *interrogative pronouns* when they are used to ask questions.

EXAMPLES:

Who is the boy in the blue sweater?

What are we going to do all summer?

Which did you choose?

NOTE: The pronoun *who* has three cases:

subjective	who	used as subject or predicate pronoun
objective	whom	used as direct object, indirect object, object of the preposition
possessive	whose	used to show ownership

HOW TO CHOOSE THE RIGHT PRONOUN: who/whom

* Relax.

   First of all, relax. Most people use *who* so much of the time in speaking, that it's now okay to ignore the rules about *who* and *whom* in speech.

   IN YOUR WRITING, HOWEVER, IT'S STILL IMPORTANT TO USE *WHO* ONLY AS A SUBJECT OR PREDICATE PRONOUN AND TO USE *WHOM* as an object. The following clues will help you out.

* Substitute another pronoun. Here's how to choose between *who* and *whom* in a question:

1. Change the question to a statement.
2. Substitute *he/him, she/her,* or *they/them* for *who/whom.*
3. If *he, she,* or *they* fit the sentence, then *who* is the right choice. If *him, her,* or *them* fit the sentence, then *whom* is the right choice.

EXAMPLE:

Who/Whom did they elect class president?

Step 1:	Change to statement:	They did elect who/whom class president.
Step 2:	Substitute *she/her:*	They did elect she/her class president.
Step 3:	*her = whom*	Whom did they elect class president?

* Cross out the interrupters.

Cross out phrases such as *did you say, I thought, I believe, does she think,* and *he said.* They are interrupters and will only confuse you.

EXAMPLE:

Who/Whom do you think will be player of the year?

Step 1:	Cross out *do you think:*	Who/Whom will be player of the year?
Step 2:	Substitute *he/him:*	He/Him will be player of the year.

| Step 3: | *he = who* | Who do you think will be player of the year? |

EXAMPLE:

Who/Whom did he say he wanted to see?

Step 1:	Cross out *did he say*:	Who/Whom he wanted to see?
Step 2:	Rewrite as statement:	He wanted to see who/whom.
Step 3:	Substitute *they/them*:	He wanted to see they/(them.)
Step 4:	*them = whom*	Whom did he say he wanted to see?

* Cross out the words before a clause.

You'll often find clauses starting with *who* or *whom* in the middle of a sentence. When you do, just cross out all the words that come before the *who* or *whom* and read the clause by itself. If the clause needs a subject, choose *who*. If the clause needs an object, choose *whom*.

EXAMPLES:

~~Open the door~~ to (whoever)/whomever gives the password.

~~I'll help~~ (whoever)/whomever asks me.

~~Ask~~ whoever/(whomever) you like.

NOTE: Once again, substituting *he/him, she/her,* or *they/them* will make your selection even easier.

HOW TO CHOOSE THE RIGHT PRONOUN:
who's/whose

This confusing pair is similar to *it's* and *its*. Just remember that, once again, the pronoun with the apostrophe is a contraction of two words:

Use *who's* when you can substitute *who is*.

EXAMPLES:

Who's there? = *Who is* there?

I like a boy *who's* always on time. = I like a boy *who is* always on time.

Use *whose* to show possession.

EXAMPLES:

Whose project did you like best?

I like a boy *whose* eyes are blue.

DEMONSTRATIVE PRONOUNS

This, that, these, and *those* are called *demonstrative pronouns* because they demonstrate or point things out. *This* and *that* are singular. *These* and *those* are plural.

* *This* and *these* are used to point out something nearby.

   That and *those* refer to things a distance away.

   EXAMPLES:

   This is the one I want.

   That is Cynthia's father across the aisle.

* *This, that, these,* and *those* may also be used as modifiers before a noun. They are then called *demonstrative adjectives*.

EXAMPLES:

This necklace once belonged to my grandmother.
Those trees next door are beautiful.

HOW TO CHOOSE THE RIGHT PRONOUN:
this/that/these/those/they/them

* **This here/that there**
  Avoid the expressions *this here, that there, these here,* and *those there.* If you use *this* and *these* to indicate things nearby, and *that* and *those* to indicate things at a distance, then the words *here* and *there* are unnecessary.

* **Those/them**
  Some people incorrectly use the word *them* as an adjective.

  REMEMBER:
  Them always stands alone. It cannot be used as a modifier before a noun. When you need a word to modify a noun, use *those.*

  EXAMPLES:
  You can say: I like *those.*
                   I like *them.*
                   I like *those* flowers.
  BUT don't say: I like *them* flowers.

* **Those/they/them**
  Some people incorrectly use the word *them* as a subject when they should use *they* or *those.* REMEMBER: *Them* is an objective case pronoun. It should never be used as a subject.

INDEFINITE PRONOUNS

Indefinite pronouns do not identify a specific person, place, or thing. The indefinite pronouns include:

everybody, everyone, nobody, none, no one, any, anybody, anyone, anything, nothing, all, both, each, enough, more, most, much, several, either, neither, few, many, less, little, another, one, two, three, etc.

EXAMPLES:

Several were missing.

Doesn't *everybody* like summer?

Both of the boys offered to help.

Two were broken.

NOTE: Some indefinite pronouns can also be used as adjectives.

EXAMPLES:

Many teenagers earn their own money.

Can you write with *either* hand?

Two chairs were broken.

NOTE: Form the possessive of indefinite pronouns by adding '*s*. When the word *else* appears after the pronoun, add the '*s* to *else*.

EXAMPLES:

someone's bike

someone else's bike

41

RECIPROCAL PRONOUNS

Reciprocal pronouns express a two-way relationship. The reciprocal pronouns are *each other* and *one another*.

EXAMPLES:

Are Pam and Jack still dating *each other*?

She believes we all should help *one another*.

NOTE: To form the possessive of a reciprocal pronoun, add *'s*.

EXAMPLES:

Sometimes Sarah and I borrow *each other's* clothes.

We really enjoy *one another's* company.

PRONOUNS AND ANTECEDENTS

The *antecedent* of a pronoun is the word or words that a pronoun refers to. The antecedent is usually a noun or pronoun. In the examples below, the arrows point to the antecedents.

EXAMPLES:

Michael scored *his* tenth run of the season.

Ask Leslie's *friends* if *they* can come.

When *Mary* and I leave, *we* will take some records.

We took *our* time getting there.

A PRONOUN SHOULD AGREE WITH ITS ANTECEDENT IN PERSON

This means that if the antecedent is in the third person, the pronoun that refers to it should also be in the third person.

EXAMPLES:

Don't say: If a *player* wants to stay on the team, *you* have to work hard.

Say: If a *player* wants to stay on the team, *he* (or *she*, if it's a girls' team) has to work hard.

A PRONOUN SHOULD AGREE WITH ITS ANTECEDENT IN NUMBER

This means that if the antecedent is singular, the pronoun that refers to it should be singular. If the antecedent is plural, the pronoun should also be plural.

EXAMPLES:

My *father* said *he* might change *his* mind.

Do *fathers* remember what *they* were like in *their* teens?

HOW TO CHOOSE THE RIGHT PRONOUN:
Singular or Plural?

* Nouns that aren't specific

PROBLEM: When a *player* on the boys' basketball team is late for practice, he/they must run laps.

CLUE: *Sometimes a noun is singular even though it doesn't refer to any one person or thing in particular.* In the sentence above, the noun *player* is singular, so the pronoun that refers to it must be singular. *He* is the right choice.

NOTE: If you don't like the sound of the singular pronoun, you can usually rewrite the whole sentence in the plural.

EXAMPLE:

When *players* on the boys' basketball team are late for practice, *they* must run laps.

* One of the . . .

PROBLEM: One of the girls left her/their mittens on the bus.

CLUE: *Don't let prepositional phrases lead you astray*. Cross them out if you need to. In the sentence above, the mittens belonged to only one girl, so *her* is the right choice:

* Nouns joined by "or"

PROBLEM: Either Tim or Jeff will lend me his/their bike.

CLUE: The antecedent is *either* the singular noun *Tim* or the singular noun *Jeff*, so *his* is the right choice.

* Collective noun acting as a unit

PROBLEM: The newspaper staff changed its/their policy on printing letters from students.

CLUE: A collective noun takes a singular pronoun when the group acts together as one unit. In the sentence above, *its* is the better choice.

* Collective noun acting as individuals

PROBLEM: The newspaper staff must turn in its/their stories to Mrs. March tomorrow.

CLUE: A collective noun takes a plural pronoun when the members of the group act as individuals. The members of the newspaper staff must write and turn in their stories individually, not as a unit. *Their* is the better choice in the sentence above.

GRAMMAR AND GENDER:
Times Are Changing

A pronoun should agree with its antecedent in gender (sex). This sometimes causes problems. When you use nouns such as *boy* or *girl*, it's easy to choose a pronoun of the right gender. But what pronoun would you use in the following sentence?

A doctor should be honest with his/her patients.

Believe it or not, there are such things as "hot issues" in grammar, and this is one of them. Until recently, the rule was simple, but times are changing.

* Traditionally, when the gender of a singular noun was not indicated, a *masculine* pronoun was used. The *he* in this case was supposed to be a "common gender" pronoun referring to either sex. Girls, as well as boys, were supposed to be included by this sentence:

A teenager can't learn to be mature unless *he* is allowed to make *his* own decisions.

45

* If you are a girl, you may very well have felt left out when you read the sentence above. If the sentence means *he or she*, why doesn't it just say so, you may ask. Sometimes both pronouns are used, but this can sound awkward, especially if the pronouns have to be repeated:

> A teenager can't learn to be mature unless *he or she* is allowed to make *his or her* own decisions. *He or she* should be given responsibilities that *he or she* can handle.

* On the other hand, if the sentence means teenagers in general, why not say so? *Making the sentence plural is sometimes your best bet.*

> Teenagers can't learn to be mature unless *they* are allowed to make *their* own decisions.

* Sometimes you can rewrite the sentence in other ways to avoid pronouns altogether:

> Being allowed to make decisions is an important step toward maturity for a teenager.

Everyone Did *His* Best?

The indefinite pronouns (*anybody, everyone, somebody*, etc.) are considered to be third person singular. They have traditionally been used with masculine pronouns.

EXAMPLES:

Everyone did *his* best to help.

If anyone asks, tell *him* the movie starts at eight o'clock.

* Once again, you may use *him or her* and *his or her*, if you like.

EXAMPLE:

Everyone did *his or her* best to help.

If anyone asks, tell *him or her* the movie starts at eight o'clock.

* Many women would actually prefer using an ungrammatical plural pronoun rather than those above.

EXAMPLES:

Everyone did *their* best to help.

If anyone asks, tell *them* the movie starts at eight o'clock.

NOTE: This usage is becoming more common, but it is still not accepted as Standard English. In your compositions, stick with *him* or *him or her*. Better still, try to rewrite your sentence to avoid the problem.

EXCEPTION: Sometimes it just doesn't make sense to use a singular pronoun to refer to *everyone*.

EXAMPLE:

Everyone must have been tired, because he fell asleep on the way home.

In informal writing, you could surely use the plural *they* in this sentence. In formal writing, you might want to rewrite the sentence to avoid the ungrammatical wording.

EXAMPLE:

All of my friends must have been tired, because they fell asleep on the way home.

BEWARE OF THE SLIPPERY PRONOUN

Make sure that every pronoun you use refers clearly and unmistakably to its antecedent. When the reference of a pronoun is unclear, the sentence can be confusing—and hilarious.

EXAMPLES:

After Jean and Sally watched the whales perform, *they* were taken to another tank and fed 100 pounds of fish.
(the girls or the whales?)

Steve told John that *his* grades were the worst in the whole school.
(Steve's grades or John's grades?)

The Spartans played the Warriors on *their* home court.
(whose home court—the Spartans' or the Warriors'?)

When a pronoun reference is unclear, you should either repeat one of the nouns or rewrite the sentence in some other way to make the meaning clear.

EXAMPLES:

After Jean and Sally watched the whales perform, *the whales* were taken to another tank and fed 100 pounds of fish.

Steve said, "John, your grades are the worst in the whole school." OR Steve said, "John, my grades are the worst in the whole school."

The Spartans played the Warriors on the Warriors' home court. OR The Spartans played the Warriors on the Spartans' home court. OR The Spartans, on their home court, played a great game against the Warriors.

OTHER PRONOUN TIPS

* Mention yourself last.
  When speaking of yourself and someone else, always mention yourself last.

  EXAMPLES:
  Bill and I, them and us, you and me

* Avoid "they say"
  The pronoun *they* should always refer to someone in particular. Avoid expressions such as *they say*, in which the meaning of *they* is unclear.

  EXAMPLES:

Don't say:	They say it's supposed to snow tomorrow.
Say:	The weatherman says it's supposed to snow tomorrow.
Don't say:	They say that kind of car is hard to drive.
Say:	I've been told that that kind of car is hard to drive.
Don't say:	They say inflation rates might go down.
Say:	The President says inflation rates might go down.

* Avoid double subjects
  Don't use unnecessary pronouns with the subject of a sentence.

  EXAMPLE:

  | Don't say: | A friend of mine he has a motorcycle. |
  | Say: | A friend of mine has a motorcycle. |

Chapter 5

ACTION!
All About Verbs

A *verb* expresses action, being, or state of being.

EXAMPLES:

The Eagles *scored* a touchdown in the third quarter.

Mark *is* here.

I *feel* tired.

NOTE: Sometimes the "action" of a verb is mental, rather than physical.

EXAMPLES:

I *dreamed* about flying saucers last night.

Do you *want* more ice cream?

VERB PHRASES

A *verb phrase* is a verb that consists of more than one word. The last word in the phrase is called the *main verb*. The other words are called *auxiliary verbs*. Auxiliary verbs are sometimes known as *helping verbs* because they help the verb to express shades of meaning or to show when an action occurred.

AUXILIARY VERBS

Here are the most common auxiliaries used in English. Sometimes two or three of them occur together in various combinations.

am, is, are, was, were, be, been
can, could
do, does, did
has, have, had
may, might, must
shall, will, should, would

EXAMPLES:

We <u>are</u> <u>making</u> Carol a birthday present.
   aux main

I <u>might</u> <u>be</u> <u>singing</u> in the talent show.
 aux aux main

You <u>should</u> <u>have</u> <u>seen</u> the first quarter of the game.
   aux   aux main

<u>Can</u> you <u>imitate</u> Steve Martin?
aux   main

NOTE: Some auxiliaries can be used as main verbs.

EXAMPLES:

She did <u>tell</u> <u>me</u> what you said.
    aux main

I <u>did</u> the dishes reluctantly.
 main

<u>Are</u> you <u>watching</u> TV?
aux   main

<u>Are</u> you sorry you missed the ending?
main

VERB TENSES: A Matter of Time

Verbs not only tell *what* happens, they also give an idea of *when* something happens. They tell whether an action or state of being is occurring in the past, present, or future. The time expressed by a verb is called its *tense*. There are six tenses in English:

present (see p. 57), *past* (see p. 59), *future* (see p. 59), *present perfect* (see p. 60), *past perfect* (see p. 61), and *future perfect* (see p. 61).

PRINCIPAL PARTS OF REGULAR VERBS

Every verb has four *principal parts* that are used to form all its tenses. These parts are: the *present infinitive*, the *present participle*, the *past*, and the *past participle*.

*The *present infinitive* usually looks the same as the present tense. It is the form of the verb you would look up in the dictionary. Normally it appears with the word *to* before it.

EXAMPLES:

(to) jump   (to) hope   (to) carry

*The *present participle* is the -*ing* form of the verb. It is used with a form of *to be* in a verb phrase, or it can be used alone in a participial phrase.

EXAMPLES:

(is) jumping   (is) hoping   (is) carrying

*The *past* of regular verbs is formed by adding *d* or *ed*.

EXAMPLES:

jumped   hoped   carried

*The *past participle* of regular verbs looks the same as the past. The past participle is always used with a form of *to have*.

EXAMPLES:

has jumped   had hoped   have carried

PRESENT INFINITIVE	PRESENT PARTICIPLE	PAST	PAST PARTICIPLE
to jump	(is) jumping	jumped	(has) jumped
to hope	(is) hoping	hoped	(has) hoped
to carry	(is) carrying	carried	(has) carried

PRINCIPAL PARTS OF IRREGULAR VERBS

Irregular verbs are verbs that do NOT form their past and past participles by adding *d* or *ed*. They change in some other way. The past and past participle of irregular verbs are usually not the same. Below is a chart of the most common irregular verbs listed in alphabetical order. When you are not sure how to form the past or past participle of an irregular verb, refer to this chart or check your dictionary. In the dictionary, the forms will be listed at the beginning of the entry, before the definition.

PRESENT INFINITIVE	PAST	PAST PARTICIPLE (used with have, has, had)
arise	arose	arisen
beat	beat	beaten or beat
become	became	become
begin	began	begun
bite	bit	bitten
blow	blew	blown
break	broke	broken
bring	brought	brought
burst	burst	burst
catch	caught	caught
choose	chose	chosen

PRESENT INFINITIVE	PAST	PAST PARTICIPLE
come	came	come
cost	cost	cost
creep	crept	crept
deal	dealt	dealt
dig	dug	dug
dive	dived or dove	dived
do	did	done
draw	drew	drawn
drink	drank	drunk
drive	drove	driven
eat	ate	eaten
fall	fell	fallen
fight	fought	fought
flee	fled	fled
fly	flew	flown
forget	forgot	forgotten
forbid	forbade	forbidden
forsake	forsook	forsaken
freeze	froze	frozen
get	got	got or gotten
give	gave	given
go	went	gone
grow	grew	grown
hang (a picture)	hung	hung
hurt	hurt	hurt
know	knew	known
lay	laid	laid

PRESENT INFINITIVE	PAST	PAST PARTICIPLE
lead	led	led
lend	lent	lent
let	let	let
lie (rest or recline)	lay	lain
lose	lost	lost
mean	meant	meant
ride	rode	ridden
ring	rang	rung
rise	rose	risen
run	ran	run
set	set	set
sit	sat	sat
see	saw	seen
shake	shook	shaken
shoot	shot	shot
show	showed	shown
shrink	shrank or shrunk	shrunk or shrunken
sing	sang	sung
sink	sank or sunk	sunk
slay	slew	slain
slide	slid	slid
speak	spoke	spoken
spring	sprang or sprung	sprung
steal	stole	stolen
string	strung	strung

PRESENT INFINITIVE	PAST	PAST PARTICIPLE
swim	swam	swum
swing	swung	swung
take	took	taken
tear	tore	torn
throw	threw	thrown
wake	waked or woke	waked or woken
win	won	won
weave	wove	woven
wring	wrung	wrung
write	wrote	written

HOW TO CHOOSE THE RIGHT PRINCIPAL PART:
Went/Gone, Saw/Seen, Came/Come

The principal parts of irregular verbs are often misused. Sometimes people are simply unfamiliar with the correct forms or are not in the habit of using them.

EXAMPLE:

I ~~brung~~ brought my lunch today.

In other cases, the speaker is familiar with all the principal parts of the verb, but carelessly uses the past instead of the past participle—or vice versa.

REMEMBER: Never use the past form after *has, have, or had*. Use the past participle ONLY after *has, have, or had*. (Of course, when the parts are the same, they are interchangeable.)

In the story below, choose the correct form of the verb in each case in which a choice is offered. *Refer to the principal parts chart if you get stuck.*

I came/come home late from football practice last night and discovered that Don, Marsha, and Kate had already went/gone to the movies without me. So I jumped into the car, went/gone to the Bijou, and searched the dark theater until I saw/seen my friends sitting in the middle of the third row. Slowly, I made my way to the front of the theater. Then I did/done my best to climb over people's knees and get to my seat. Have you ever did/done that?

I finally got to my seat and plopped down with relief. Unfortunately, Marsha hadn't saw/seen me coming—and I hadn't saw/seen her tub of Mr. Giant hot buttered popcorn sitting in my seat. As the tub of popcorn crumpled beneath me, I jumped up in surprise and let out a disgusted moan. Everyone in the theater turned to look at me. But Marsha just smiled. "If you had came/come on time, you wouldn't have butter all over the seat of your jeans," she said.

THE PRESENT TENSE

The *present tense* usually expresses an action that is taking place in the present—NOW.

EXAMPLES:

I *see* Andrea across the street. She probably *wants* to talk to us.

OTHER USES OF THE PRESENT TENSE

* The present tense is used to express a *customary* or *habitual* action—one which is not necessarily happening now, but which happens again and again.

EXAMPLES:

Steve's band *practices* in our garage on Saturdays.

I *see* Andrea at the movies every week. She usually *wants* to go out for a pizza afterward.

* The present tense is also used to express scientific facts and other statements that are *always* true.

EXAMPLES:

Water *freezes* at 32° F.

There *are* 60 seconds in a minute.

* Sometimes the present tense is used to express a future action.

EXAMPLE:

I *leave* for Camp Lone Star in the morning.

* Newspapers use the present tense in headlines to make the news sound more immediate and exciting.

EXAMPLE:

EARTHQUAKE ROCKS CALIFORNIA

**WRITING TIP:
Use the Present
Tense in Book
Reports and
Essay Questions**

Always use the present tense to explain what happens in a novel or other work of literature. (The events of a novel happen again and again each time someone reads the book.)

EXAMPLES:

In Chapter 6 of *Pardon Me, You're Stepping on My Eyeball!* Marsh Mellow and Edna Shingle-box *meet* for the first time.

In Act V, Romeo *finds* Juliet asleep, *thinks* she *is* dead, and *kills* himself.

NOTE: Also use the present tense to describe the techniques and style that an author uses.

EXAMPLES:

In *Pardon Me, You're Stepping on My Eyeball!* Paul Zindel *captures* the way teenagers think and feel.

In Act V, Shakespeare *creates* a stunning, tragic climax.

THE PAST TENSE

The *past tense* is used to express an action that began and ended in the past. It is often used to indicate something that happened at a definite time in the past.

EXAMPLE:

I *saw* Andrea yesterday. She *asked* to borrow my sweater.

THE FUTURE TENSE

The *future tense* is used to express an action that will take place in the future.

EXAMPLES:

I *will see* you tomorrow.

We *will bring* our records to the dance.

THE PRESENT PERFECT TENSE

The *present perfect tense* = *has* or *have* + the *past participle*.

EXAMPLES:

I *have decided* to try out for cheerleading.

She *has* often *tried* to reach you.

When to Use the Present Perfect

*Use the present perfect to express an action that began in the past but continues into the present— or an action that is completed at the moment of speaking.

EXAMPLES:

We *have* just *seen* this movie for the third time.

She *has been* in Florida for six months and wants to stay forever.

*Use the present perfect to express an action that took place at an *indefinite* time in the past.

EXAMPLES:

We *have seen* that movie before.

She *has been* to Florida many times.

NOTE: Do not use the present perfect to express an action that took place at a *definite* time in the past. Use the past tense instead.

Don't say: She *has been* in Florida last year.

     Say: She *was* in Florida last year.

Don't say: We *have seen* that movie yesterday.

     Say: We *saw* that movie yesterday.

THE PAST PERFECT TENSE

The *past perfect tense* = *had* + the *past participle*.

EXAMPLES:

I had gone, you had wanted

When to Use the Past Perfect

* Use the past perfect tense to show that one past action took place *before* another past action.

EXAMPLES:

By the time the movie started, my little brother *had* already *eaten* three candy bars.
(The *eating* took place before the *starting*.)

I *had* never *heard* the album until Jean bought it yesterday.
(The state of *not having heard* occurred before the *buying*.)

He *had* already *taken* the motorcycle apart before he realized he couldn't possibly fix it.
(The *taking apart* occurred before the *realizing*.)

THE FUTURE PERFECT TENSE

The *future perfect tense* = *will have* or *shall have* + the *past participle*.

When to Use the Future Perfect

* The future perfect tense is used to show that an action will take place *by* or *before* some definite time in the future.

EXAMPLES:

By the time school starts, I *will have saved* $200.

The next time you see me, I *will have lost* ten pounds.

PROGRESSIVE FORMS OF TENSES

Each of the six verb tenses has a *progressive* or *continuous* form. This form shows that an action is *in progress* at the time referred to in the sentence. The progressive forms = a form of the verb *to be* + a *present participle*.

EXAMPLES:

present progressive:
Jim *is jogging* right now. He hopes to make the track team in the spring.

past progressive:
He *was jogging* last night when I tried to call him.

future progressive:
I'm sure he *will be jogging* when I try to call him tonight.

present perfect progressive:
It seems as though he *has been jogging* ever since I met him.

past perfect progressive:
If he *had*n't *been jogging* on Saturday night, we would have come to your party.

future perfect progressive:
By the time track season starts, he *will have been jogging* for six months straight.

EMPHATIC FORMS

The present tense and the past tense also have *emphatic* forms. The emphatic form = *do, does,* or *did* + the *present infinitive*.

EXAMPLES:

I did see, you do not see, we don't want

* The emphatic forms are used in three ways:

For emphasis:

I *did* call you last night.

We *do* have a right to ask why.

To ask questions:

Do you know where Peter is?

For making negative statements:

He doesn't want to miss the last episode.

I do not know the answer.

USING TENSES CORRECTLY

* Shifting tenses

Don't shift from the past to the present in the middle of telling a story (unless you're quoting someone's exact words or have some other very good reason). Note the corrections made in the story below.

Last night I took Sally out to Big Burger. We had a great time . . . until dessert.

"Listen," she ~~says~~ **said** to me, as she ~~puts~~ **put** away a double hot fudge sundae. "I've been thinking about you and me."

I ~~know I'm~~ **knew I was** in trouble right away. "What about us?" I gulp.

"I think it's time we both went on a diet," she ~~sighs~~ **sighed**.

NOTE: Sometimes it is correct to change tenses, even in the middle of a sentence. Just make sure that the time relationships in the sentence make sense.

EXAMPLE:

I *found* out yesterday that the drama club *is planning* to do a new play and *will hold* try-outs next week.

* She said that . . .

A verb following the expressions *she said that, we believed that, he thought that,* etc., may be in the past tense, even if the action it refers to is in the present or future.

EXAMPLES:

You can say: She said that we *were* driving to the beach tomorrow.

Or you can say: She said that we *are* driving to the beach tomorrow.

NOTE: This rule applies even if the word *that* is understood, but not expressed.

EXAMPLES:

She said we were driving to the beach tomorrow.

She said we are driving to the beach tomorrow.

* Scientific facts

Something that is *always* true is *always* expressed in the present tense, even if it follows a verb in the past tense.

EXAMPLES:

Don't say: Isaac Newton discovered that every action *had* an equal and opposite reaction.

Say: Isaac Newton discovered that every action *has* an equal and opposite reaction.

* Present or present perfect?
Don't use the present tense to express an action that began in the past, even if the action continues into the present. Use the present perfect instead.

EXAMPLES:

Don't say: *I'm going* to this school for three years already.

Say: *I have been going* to this school for three years already.

* Could of/should of
Never use the word *of* as an auxiliary verb after *could, should, would, may, might, must,* or *ought.* This mistake is often made because contractions such as *should've* and *might've* sound so much like *should of* and *might of.*

EXAMPLES:

Don't say: You *should of* seen George in his chicken costume.

Say: You *should have* seen George in his chicken costume.

Or say: You *should've* seen George in his chicken costume.

* Had/would have
In clauses beginning with *if* and in wishes referring to the past, use *had,* not *would have.* (And NEVER use *would of.*)

EXAMPLES:

Don't say: If he would of listened to me, he wouldn't of taken such a chance.

Say: If he *had* listened to me, he *wouldn't have* taken such a chance.

Don't say: I wish I *would have* learned to ski.

Say: I wish I *had* learned to ski.

NOTE: Remember, once again, that *of* is never an auxiliary verb. Never use it after *had*.

EXAMPLES:

Don't say: If he *had of* listened, I would have explained.

Don't say: If *he'd of* listened, I would have explained.

Say: If he *had* listened, I would have explained.

Or say: If *he'd* listened, I would have explained.

VERB CONJUGATION

A verb *conjugation* is a complete list of the forms of the verb in all its tenses. Below is a conjugation of the verb *to throw*. (NOTE: This conjugation is for the active voice only.)

present tense

I throw	we throw
you throw	you throw
he	they throw
she } throws	
it	

present progressive tense

I am throwing	we are throwing
you are throwing	you are throwing
he	they are throwing
she } is throwing	
it	

present perfect tense

I have thrown	we have thrown
you have thrown	you have thrown
he }	they have thrown
she } has thrown	
it }	

present perfect progressive tense

I have been throwing	we have been throwing
you have been throwing	you have been throwing
he }	they have been throwing
she } has been throwing	
it }	

past tense

I threw	we threw
you threw	you threw
he }	they threw
she } threw	
it }	

past progressive tense

I was throwing	we were throwing
you were throwing	you were throwing
he }	they were throwing
she } was throwing	
it }	

past perfect tense

I had thrown	we had thrown
you had thrown	you had thrown
he }	they had thrown
she } had thrown	
it }	

past perfect progressive tense

I had been throwing	we had been throwing
you had been throwing	you had been throwing
he she it } had been throwing	they had been throwing

future tense

I will throw	we will throw
you will throw	you will throw
he she it } will throw	they will throw

future progressive tense

I will be throwing	we will be throwing
you will be throwing	you will be throwing
he she it } will be throwing	they will be throwing

future perfect tense

I will have thrown	we will have thrown
you will have thrown	you will have thrown
he she it } will have thrown	they will have thrown

I will have been throwing	we will have been throwing
you will have been throwing	you will have been throwing
he $\Big\}$ she $\Big\}$ will have been it $\Big\}$ throwing	they will have been throwing

TRANSITIVE OR INTRANSITIVE?

Action verbs can be *transitive* or *intransitive*, depending on how they are used in a sentence.

* A *transitive* verb passes its action on to a *direct object*. The direct object tells *who* or *what* receives the action or is affected by the action. It is usually a noun or pronoun. (EXCEPTION: See "Passive Voice," p. 76.)

EXAMPLES:

McGraw hit the ball into center field.
(Hit what? *Ball* receives the action. It is the direct object of the transitive verb *hit*.)

We painted our house.
(Painted what? *House* receives the action. It is the direct object of the transitive verb *painted*.)

I saw Julie at the fair.
(Saw whom? *Julie* receives the action. It is the direct object of the transitive verb *saw*.)

NOTE: Because the direct object completes the meaning of the sentence, it is called a completer or *complement*. For more information on complements, see p. 14.

* An *intransitive* verb does not have a direct object. There is no word in the sentence that tells who or what received the action.

EXAMPLES:

It rained all night long.

(*All night long* is a modifier that tells when. There is no word that tells who or what it rained. The verb *rained* is almost always intransitive.)

The bell rang.

I ran around the block.

(*Around the block* is a prepositional phrase used as an adverb to tell where.)

NOTE: Most action verbs can be *either* transitive or intransitive, depending on how they are used in a sentence.

EXAMPLES:

Transitive:	I wrote my report.
Intransitive:	Jill writes very well.
Transitive:	Frank was driving a new car.
Intransitive:	He drives carefully.
Transitive:	I rang the bell.
Intransitive:	The bell rang.

HOW TO CHOOSE THE RIGHT VERB:
lie/lay, sit/set, rise/raise

These verbs are misused so often that the correct uses may actually "sound funny" to you. That's why the best way to start using the verbs correctly is to practice saying the sample sentences in each section until they start sounding natural to you. After all, that's the way we learn most of our grammar—good or bad. Certain ways of speaking "sound right" to us because we're used to hearing them. If you get used to hearing yourself say: "I'm going to lie down," maybe you'll even start a correct usage fad!

LIE or LAY?

LIE

*means *to rest* or *recline* (also to remain or be situated)

never takes a direct object

*has the following principal parts:

PRESENT INFINITIVE	PRESENT PARTICIPLE
lie	(is) lying

PAST	PAST PARTICIPLE
lay	(has) lain

LAY

*means *to put* or *place* (something)

*usually takes a direct object: a word that tells *what* was placed

*has the following principal parts:

PRESENT INFINITIVE	PRESENT PARTICIPLE
lay	(is) laying

PAST	PAST PARTICIPLE
laid	(has) laid

USAGE SAMPLES

LIE

present:

If you feel tired, *lie* down and take a nap.

I wonder what *lies* buried at the bottom of my closet.

present progressive:

Mother *is lying* down because she has a headache.

Your scarf *is lying* on the floor in your room.

past:

Last summer we *lay* on the beach every day.

Last night I *lay* down at nine o'clock and fell asleep.

The books *lay* unopened on my desk for two weeks.

present perfect:

I *have lain* in bed all morning making plans.

These dirty sneakers *have lain* in my locker all semester.

LAY (something)

present:

Lay the baby down gently.

present progressive:

I *was laying* new tiles in the kitchen when you called.

past:

I *laid* my packages on the kitchen counter and sat down.

present perfect:

I *have laid* my cards on the table.

RAISE or RISE?

RAISE

*usually means to move *something* upward (also means to grow plants or animals)

*always has a direct object

*has the following principal parts:

PRESENT INFINITIVE	PRESENT PARTICIPLE
raise	(is) raising
PAST	PAST PARTICIPLE
raised	(has) raised

RISE

*means to go upward

*never takes a direct object

*has the following principal parts:

PRESENT INFINITIVE	PRESENT PARTICIPLE
rise	(is) rising
PAST	PAST PARTICIPLE
rose	(has) risen

USAGE SAMPLES

RAISE (something)

present:
Raise the shade and let in some light.

present progressive:
I *am raising* African violets.

past:

I *raised* my hand when I finally knew one of the answers.

present perfect:

He *has raised* an important question.

RISE

present:

The sun *rises* at 7:05 today.

present progressive:

The noise level in this room *is rising* quickly.

past:

The bread dough *rose* over the side of the pan.

present perfect:

My favorite song *has risen* to the number-one spot on the charts.

SIT or SET?

SIT

*means to take a seat (or be situated)

never takes a direct object

*has the following principal parts:

PRESENT INFINITIVE	PRESENT PARTICIPLE
sit	(is) sitting
PAST	PAST PARTICIPLE
sat	(has) sat

SET

*means to put or place (something)

*takes a direct object that tells *what* is put or placed

*has the following principal parts:

PRESENT INFINITIVE	PRESENT PARTICIPLE
set	(is) setting
PAST	PAST PARTICIPLE
set	(has) set

USAGE SAMPLES

SIT (never takes a direct object)

present:

Sit down and relax.

present progressive:

Joan *is sitting* in the third row.

past:

My dog *sat* there patiently.

present perfect:

Your skates *have sat* on the back steps for two weeks.

SET (something)

present:

Set the alarm for seven-thirty.

present progressive:

I *am setting* the table.

past:

I tried to carry the heavy bag, but quickly *set* it down.

present perfect:

I have *set* the cake on the table to cool.

EXCEPTION: The sun *is setting* in the west. (This is one case in which *set* does not have a direct object.)

ACTIVE or PASSIVE?

Transitive verbs are most often used in the *active voice.* This means that the *subject* of the sentence *does* the action, and the direct object receives the effect of the action.

EXAMPLE:

McGraw hit the ball into center field.
(The subject McGraw does the action.)

Transitive verbs may also be used in the *passive voice.* This means that the *receiver* of the action becomes the subject of the sentence. The doer of the action may or may not be mentioned.

EXAMPLE:

The ball was hit into center field.
(The subject *ball* receives the action. The doer of the action is not mentioned.)

The ball was hit into center field by McGraw.
(The doer of the action is mentioned in a prepositional phrase.)

NOTE: The *passive voice* = a form of the verb *to be* + a *past participle*.

USING ACTIVE and PASSIVE VOICE

*When to use the passive voice
Use the passive voice when you want to emphasize the *receiver* of the action rather than the doer—or when the doer is unknown.

EXAMPLES:

My stereo *was made* in Japan.

A mysterious package *had been left* on our doorstep.

The ransom *will be paid* tomorrow.

---

*When to use the active voice
  Use the active voice when you want to emphasize the doer of the action.

EXAMPLES:

passive—okay: Something *should have been done* by Mayor Smith!

active—better: Mayor Smith *should have done* something!

passive—okay: The decision *will be made* by me.

active—better: I *will make* the decision.

NOTE: In general, try to use the active voice as much as possible in your writing. In most cases, it will sound more lively and interesting.

LINKING VERBS

A *linking verb* does not express action. It simply links the subject to a noun, pronoun, or adjective in the predicate. The general name for the words linked to the subject is *subject complement*.

SUBJECT COMPLEMENTS

*A noun that follows a linking verb and identifies the subject is called a *predicate noun.*

EXAMPLE:

Helen is my best *friend*.

*A pronoun that follows a linking verb and identifies the subject is called a *predicate pronoun*.

EXAMPLE:

The winners of the dance contest were *he* and *she*.

NOTE: Predicate nouns and predicate pronouns are both known as *predicate nominatives*.

*An adjective that follows a linking verb and describes the subject is called a *predicate adjective*.

EXAMPLE:

The dragon was *green, enormous,* and *unfriendly*.

COMMON LINKING VERBS

*The most common linking verbs are all the forms of the verb *to be* (*am, is, are, was, were, has been, will be,* etc.).

EXAMPLES:

$\underset{\text{S}}{\text{We}} \underset{\text{L.V.}}{\text{were}}$ the only $\underset{\text{P.N.}}{\text{teenagers}}$ in the audience.

$\underset{\text{S}}{\text{Mark}} \underset{\text{L.V.}}{\text{has been}}$ really $\underset{\text{P.A.}}{\text{helpful}}$.

NOTE: Remember that the forms of the verb *to be* are not always linking verbs. Sometimes they are *auxiliary* verbs in a verb phrase. (see p. 57). Notice how the linking verbs above are used as auxiliary verbs below.

EXAMPLES:

We $\underset{\text{aux}}{\text{were}} \underset{\text{main}}{\text{trying}}$ to act calm.

Mark $\underset{\text{aux}}{\text{has}} \underset{\text{aux}}{\text{been}} \underset{\text{main}}{\text{helping}}$ me.

*Other linking verbs include:

LOOK	You *look* happy.
SOUND	That *sounds* fantastic.
FEEL	I was *feeling* depressed until you called.
TASTE	This spaghetti *tastes* good.
SMELL	Something *smelled* funny.
GROW	I am *growing* more confident about math.

REMAIN	Sally *will remain* the editor of the school paper.
APPEAR	Everything *appeared* normal.
BECOME	That show *is becoming* popular. Will you *become* an artist?
SEEM	Rebecca *seems* nervous about something.

NOTE: Most linking verbs can also be used as action verbs, either transitive or intransitive. Note the different uses of the verbs below.

CLUE: Usually, if you can substitute a form of *to be* for the verb, it is a linking verb.

EXAMPLES:

Linking:

The roast beef *tastes* delicious.

(*Delicious* is a predicate adjective describing *roast beef*.)

You could say: The roast beef *is* delicious.

Action:

She *tasted* the roast beef.

(*Roast beef* is the direct object of the action verb *tasted*.)

You could not say: She *was* the roast beef.

Linking:

Sam *looked* ready to leave.

(*Ready* is a predicate adjective describing *Sam*.)

You could say: Sam *was* ready to leave.

Action:

Sam *looked* everywhere for his new Frisbee.

(*Looked* tells what Sam did. It is an action verb.)

You could not say: Sam *was* everywhere for his new Frisbee.

Linking:

Have you ever *felt* lonely?

(*Lonely* is a predicate adjective describing *you*.)

You could say: Have you ever *been* lonely?

Action:

Have you ever *felt* sandpaper?

(*Sandpaper* is the direct object of the action verb *felt*.)

You could not say: Have you ever *been* sandpaper?

SUBJECTS AND VERBS SHOULD ALWAYS AGREE!

A singular subject takes a singular verb. A plural subject takes a plural verb. It sounds simple, right? But making subjects and verbs match is one of the biggest problems most people have with the English language. That's why it's probably a good idea to review the rules in this section before you turn in a composition. You might see fewer red marks on your paper when you get it back.

REMEMBER:

* A *singular* subject takes a *singular* verb.

   A *plural* subject takes a *plural* verb.

* A *singular* verb ends in *s* (unless the subject is *I* or *you*).

   A *plural* verb does *not* end in *s*. As you know, the opposite is true for nouns.

EXAMPLES:

singular subject and verb: The cost seems too high.

plural subject and verb: The costs seem too high.

HOW TO MAKE SUBJECTS
AND VERBS AGREE

IGNORE OTHER PARTS
OF THE SENTENCE

* Ignore prepositional phrases.
Never look for the subject in a prepositional phrase.

EXAMPLES:

The *cost* ~~of records~~ *seems* to be going up.

The *mysteries* ~~of outer space~~ *are* being probed by astronauts.

EXCEPTION: When the subject is *most, some, all, any, none,* or a fraction such as *half* or *two thirds*, you should pay attention to the prepositional phrase that follows. See "Problem Pronouns," p. 88.

* Ignore nouns and pronouns in the predicate.
Sometimes the subject is singular, but the predicate noun or pronoun is plural—or vice versa. REMEMBER: The verb always agrees with the subject.

EXAMPLES:

My greatest *love is* still cartoons.
Cartoons are still my greatest love.

TWO OR MORE SUBJECTS

* Compound subjects joined by AND
Compound subjects joined by *and* usually take a plural verb.

EXAMPLES:

My mother and father *are coming* to the play.

EXCEPTION #1: When two nouns joined by *and* refer to one person or thing, they take a singular verb.

EXAMPLES:

Macaroni and cheese *is* my favorite meal. (one dish)

My next-door neighbor and best friend *is* Pam. (one person)

EXCEPTION #2: When nouns joined by *and* are modified by *each*, *every*, or *many a*, they take a singular verb.

EXAMPLES:

Every car and motorcycle *needs* a license.

Each student and teacher *is* being asked to sell five candy bars.

* Compound subjects joined by OR
Singular subjects joined by *or* or *nor* take a singular subject.

EXAMPLE:

Either the singer or the dancer *is* on next.

When one subject is singular and the other is plural, the verb agrees with the subject that is closer to it.

EXAMPLES:

Either the singer or the *dancers are* on next.

Either the dancers or the *singer is* on next.

HAVE IT YOUR WAY: If the two sentences above sound awkward, you can rewrite them as follows.

EXAMPLES:

Either the singer *is* on next, or the dancers *are*.

Either the dancers *are* on next, or the singer
is.

* Nouns joined by *together with, along with*
Nouns joined by phrases such as *together
with, along with, in addition to, as well as,* and
accompanied by do NOT make a compound
subject. Only the first noun is the subject.

EXAMPLES:

The *tempo* of the song, as well as the words,
was all wrong.

Cold *weather*, in addition to moisture, *is* caus-
ing the problem.

Marsha, along with Terry, *plays* tennis well.

HAVE IT YOUR WAY: If these sentences
"sound funny" to you, you can usually
change the phrases to *and*. Then use a plural
verb.

EXAMPLES:

The tempo and the words of the song *were*
all wrong.

Marsha and Tony *play* tennis well.

* Affirmative vs. Negative
When one subject is affirmative and the
other is negative, the verb always agrees
with the affirmative one.

EXAMPLE:

You, not I, *are* to blame.

HAVE IT YOUR WAY: Once again, if this
kind of sentence sounds awkward to you,
you can usually rewrite it.

EXAMPLE:

You are to blame, not I.

SPECIAL NOUNS

* Singular nouns that end in *s*
Some nouns that end is *s* are actually singular and take a singular verb.

EXAMPLES:

No *news is* good news.

Measles is a common disease.

NOTE: Some nouns that always end in *s* can be either singular or plural, depending on how they are used in a sentence. Check your dictionary to find out which meanings are considered singular and which meanings are considered plural.

EXAMPLES:

Acoustics *is* the study of sound.
The acoustics in the auditorium *are* terrible.

OTHER EXAMPLES: statistics, politics

* Nouns that are always plural
Some nouns are always plural. They do not have a singular form.

EXAMPLES:

These *jeans are* my favorites.

Those *scissors are* not sharp enough.

EXCEPTION: When we say *a pair of jeans* or *a pair of scissors*, the word *pair* is the subject. It takes a singular verb.

EXAMPLES:

This *pair* of jeans *is* my favorite.

This *pair* of scissors *is* not sharp enough.

* Collective nouns
A collective noun is one that names a group

or collection of things. It can be either singular or plural, depending on how it is used in a sentence.

When the group as a whole is acting as a single unit, use a singular verb.

EXAMPLES:

Every time the clown appears, the *audience roars* with laughter.

The basketball *team plays* its first game tonight.

When the members of the group are acting as individuals, use a plural verb.

EXAMPLES:

The *audience were* already putting on their coats.

The basketball *team invite* their parents to every game.

HAVE IT YOUR WAY: If the sentences above sound awkward, you can rewrite them by inserting the word *members* in each one.

EXAMPLES:

The *members* of the audience *were* already putting on their coats.

The *members* of the basketball team *invite* their parents to every game.

NOTE: Also see "How to Choose the Right Pronoun: Singular or Plural?" pp. 44–45.

NOTE: Also see "How to Choose the Right Pronoun: Singular or Plural?" pp. 44–45.

* Nouns of amount

  When a plural noun names an amount of something—time, money, weight, etc.—it takes a *singular* verb.

EXAMPLES:

Seven dollars *is* a reasonable price.

Two hours *is* too long to wait.

Ten pounds of potatoes *is* not enough.

*Titles

The title of one particular thing always takes a singular verb, even if the title contains plural words.

EXAMPLES:

Star Wars is still my favorite movie.

Crime and Punishment is a fascinating novel.

*The number is/a number are

The number = *the total* or *the quantity*. It means a specific number such as 6 or 84. It takes a singular verb.

A number = *several, many*. It takes a plural verb.

EXAMPLES:

The number of gold records *is* decreasing.

A number of gold records *were* played on the radio last night.

TURNED-AROUND SENTENCES

*There is/there are

Watch out for sentences that begin with *here* or *there*. These words are NEVER the subject of a sentence. The subject usually comes *after* the verb in these sentences. You must think ahead to what the subject is going to be before you choose the right verb.

EXAMPLES:

Don't say: There's three reasons I want the Phillies to win.

    Say: There are three reasons I want the Phillies to win.
(The verb agrees with the plural subject *reasons*.)

    Say: There's a bag of peanuts in the cupboard. (The verb agrees with the singular subject *bag*.)

Don't say: Here's your knife and fork.

    Say: Here are your knife and fork.
(The verb agrees with two subjects joined by *and*.)

    Say: There was a drawing or a photo on each page of the book.
(Two singular subjects joined by *or* take a singular verb.)

* Questions

In a question, part of the verb usually comes before the subject. Again, you have to think ahead to the subject before you can pick the right form of the verb.

EXAMPLES:

Don't say: Where's the bananas?

    Say: Where are the bananas?
(The verb agrees with the plural suject *bananas*.)

Don't say: Was there enough tomatoes on your sandwich?

    Say: Were there enough tomatoes on your sandwich?
(The verb agrees with the plural subject *tomatoes*.)

Don't say:	Do either of those answers sound right?
Say:	Does either of those answers sound right?

(The verb agrees with the singular subject *either*. Ignore the prepositional phrase *of those answers*.)

* Other turned-around sentences

There are other kinds of sentences in which the verb comes before the subject. When you are talking, no one is going to pay that much attention to whether you choose the right verb in a long, complicated sentence. But when you are writing, take the time to find the subject of the sentence and make the verb agree.

EXAMPLES:

At the end of the movie *come* the *credits*.

Between the topping and the crust *was* a *layer* of marshmallows.

PROBLEM PRONOUNS

* Pronouns that are always singular

The pronouns *each*, *either*, *neither*, *every*, *everyone*, *everybody*, *anybody*, *anyone*, *anything*, *nobody*, *one*, *somebody*, *someone*, and *something* ALWAYS take a singular verb.

EXAMPLES:

Each of the thermoses *holds* the same amount.

Everyone is glad to see you.

* Pronouns that are always plural

The pronouns *both*, *few*, *others*, *many*, and *several* ALWAYS take a plural verb.

EXAMPLES:

Both of the answers *were* right.

* Pronouns that can be either singular or plural
The words *most of, some of, all of, part of, enough of, none of,* and *any of* may be either singular or plural, depending on the word that follows *of*. When the word following *of* is singular, use a singular verb. When the word following *of* is plural, use a plural verb. The same rule holds true for fractions such as *half* or *two thirds*.

EXAMPLES:

Most of the seats *were* already gone.

Most of the cake *was* already gone.

Are any of your friends going?

Is any of the money yours?

None of my friends *are* going.

None of the money *is* mine.

* More than one
Believe it or not, the expression *more than one* takes a singular verb.

EXAMPLES:

More than one person *has realized* that this doesn't make sense.

* One of those who
The verb following *one of those who* is almost always plural, because *who* usually refers to the plural noun that comes right before it, not to *one*.

EXAMPLES:

John is *one of those boys who like* gym class.
(This sentence really means: Of those boys who like gym class, John is one.)

EXCEPTION: The words *the only* can make a big difference in a sentence like this.

EXAMPLE:

John is the only one of those boys who *likes* gym class.

(This sentence really means: Of those boys, John is the only one who likes gym class.)

* I who am

I, who am the oldest, *have* the most responsibility. Although this sentence may "sound funny" to you, it is correct because a verb following *who* must always agree with the word that *who* refers to—in this case *I*.

* If I was/If I were/I wish I were

When you are expressing a wish or an idea contrary to fact, use *if I were,* or *I wish I were.* In this case, the word *were* is not plural. It is a very special instance called the subjunctive mood.

EXAMPLES:

a wish:	*I wish I were* going.
an idea contrary to fact:	*If I were* taller, I could play basketball.
BUT for a simple past action:	*If I was* rude to you, I'm sorry.

BAD HABITS

* He doesn't or he don't?

He do not like tomatoes. Does that sentence sound right to you? Probably not. But how about this one? *He don't like tomatoes.* Chances are, it sounds okay to you because the word *don't* is misused so often. REMEMBER: *Don't* is a contraction of the words *do not*. When you cannot substitute the words *do not*, use *doesn't*, which means *does not*. If you have a bad case of *he don't*, the only cure is practice. The more you hear yourself say *he doesn't*, the more natural it will sound to you.

EXAMPLES:

He doesn't like liver.

It doesn't matter.

Doesn't she want to enter the contest?

Doesn't he understand my problem?

This pen doesn't work.

*You was/you were

Some people also have a bad habit of saying *you was* instead of you were. *You were* is always the right choice.

*Am I not?/Aren't I?/Ain't I?

Don't say: Ain't I?

Say: Aren't I? or Am I not?

NOTE: Nobody feels comfortable using these expressions, so whenever you can, rephrase your question to avoid them altogether.

VERBS USED AS OTHER PARTS OF SPEECH

A *verbal* is a verb form that can be used as another part of speech. There are three kinds of verbals: *participles, gerunds,* and *infinitives.*

PARTICIPLES

The Present Participle

The *present participle* is the *-ing* form of the verb. It can be used as an *adjective*.

NOTE: A *participial phrase* is a group of related words containing a participle. In a participial phrase, the whole phrase acts as an adjective.

Present Participles Used as Adjectives

before a noun:
What a *relaxing* day this is.
(describes day, tells what kind)

after a linking verb:
This music is *relaxing*.
(describes music)

in a participial phrase:
Jean is the girl *wearing the red dress*.
(the entire phrase describes girl, tells which one)
The plants *growing on the windowsill* are mine.
(the entire phrase describes plants, tells which ones)

The Past Participle

The *past participle* is the form of the verb normally used with *have* or *has*. It often, but not always, ends in *ed*. The past participle can also be used as an adjective.

Past Participles Used as Adjectives

before a noun:
I like *fried* chicken.
(describes chicken, tells what kind)

after a linking verb:

Jim seems *relaxed*.
(describes Jim)

in a participial phrase:

The costumes *worn at the party* were very imaginative.
(describes costumes, tells which ones)

Relaxed by the warm atmosphere and friendly people, Jim began to circulate.
(the entire phrase describes Jim)

The Perfect Participle

There is a third kind of participle, not used as often as the other two. It is called the *perfect participle*. The perfect participle = *having + the past participle*. It, too, can be used as an adjective.

EXAMPLES:

Having made up my mind, I felt better.
(describes *I*)

The pitcher, *having completed his windup*, followed through with a terrific fast ball.
(describes *pitcher*)

ADJECTIVE OR VERB?

Participles Used After *To Be*
A participle that follows a form of the verb *to be* is sometimes an adjective and sometimes part of a verb phrase.

*The *present participle* can either describe a noun or help express an action in progress.

adjective: This music is *relaxing*.
(no action; just describes the noun *music*)

verb: Jim *is relaxing* on the beach.
(action in progress; tells what Jim is doing)

NOTE: *-Ing* words that act as *nouns* are called gerunds. See p. 95.

* The *past participle* can also describe a noun or help express an action.

adjective: The carpet on the stairs was dirty and *worn*.
(describes the carpet)

verb: The dress *was worn* by Jane.
(expresses an action)

PUNCTUATION POINTERS:
When to Use Commas with a Participial Phrase

* When a participial phrase is *essential* to the meaning of the sentence, *do not* set it off with commas.

EXAMPLES:

Give the package to a man *carrying three blue roses and eating a cheeseburger*.

(Without the participial phrases, the essential message of the sentence would be lost.)

* When the participial phrase is *not essential* to the sentence, *set it off with commas* to show that it supplies extra information that interrupts the main message of the sentence.

EXAMPLE:

My father, *exhausted after a long day*, fell asleep at the dinner table.

*When a participial phrase *begins* a sentence, *always* use a comma after it.

EXAMPLES:

no comma: Disneyland is a world-famous resort *located in California.*

comma: *Located in California*, Disneyland is a world-famous resort.

GERUNDS

When the *-ing* form of the verb is used as a noun, it is called a *gerund*. A gerund can do the same jobs that a noun does in a sentence.

gerund as subject:
Swimming is fun.

gerund as direct object:
He hates *studying*.

gerund as predicate nominative:
My favorite activity is *running*.

gerund as object of preposition:
I'm tired of *practicing*.

gerund as indirect object:
I always give *eating* my full attention.

USE THE POSSESSIVE CASE
BEFORE A GERUND

A personal pronoun or a noun that names a person is usually in the possessive case when it comes before a gerund.

EXAMPLES:

Nancy's singing is absolutely beautiful.

Your forgetting my phone number was a disaster!

Nobody minded *my asking* so many questions.

We were sad about *his leaving* so suddenly.

REMEMBER: Not all *-ing* words are gerunds. Some are participles. See p. 92.

INFINITIVES

The Present Infinitive

The ***present infinitive*** is the form of the verb you would look up in the dictionary. Used in a sentence as a part of speech, it usually follows the word *to*.

* Infinitives can be used as *nouns*, *adjectives*, or *adverbs*.

EXAMPLES:

noun—subject:

To complain is a waste of time.

noun—direct object:

Do you like *to dance*?

noun—predicate nominative:

My ambition is *to invent* a time machine.

adjective:

I know an easier way *to do* that.

adverb:

I was glad *to see* you.

He went upstairs *to find* it.

The Perfect Infinitive

The *perfect infinitive* = *to have* + the *past participle*.
It is used to refer to something that happened *before*
the action of the main verb.

EXAMPLES:

present infinitive:

I seem *to need* a new umbrella.

perfect infinitive:

I seem *to have lost* the old one.

perfect infinitive:

I am sorry *to have missed* the concert.

TIPS ON USING INFINITIVES

Never use the perfect infinitive after a main
verb that already contains *have* or *had*. Use the
present infinitive instead.

Don't say:	I *had hoped to have seen* you before you left.
Say:	I *had hoped to see* you before you left.
Don't say:	I *would have liked to have done* better.
Say:	I *would have liked to do* better.
Or say:	I *would like to have done* better.

*Split Infinitives

It's okay to "split" an infinitive once in a while by putting a word or words between *to* and the verb. Just make sure that splitting the infinitive is the best way to say what you want to say—and make sure that the split isn't too wide!

EXAMPLES:

okay:

To *really* enjoy mountain climbing, a person has to like taking risks.

(There's no other place to put *really*.)

not so good:

The pilot had to *manually* take over the controls.

(There's a better place to put *manually*.)

better:

The pilot had to take over the controls *manually*.

terrible:

I want to *as long as you don't mind* ask Mary to the dance.

better:

I want to ask Mary to the dance, *as long as you don't mind*.

Chapter 6

TO BE EXACT:
All About Adjectives, Adverbs, and Prepositions

A *modifier* tells more about another word. There are two main kinds of modifiers: *adjectives* and *adverbs*.

ADJECTIVES

An *adjective* modifies—tells more about—a noun or pronoun. It tells *what kind, how many,* or *which one*. Here are the kinds of words that modify nouns. Some of them can also modify pronouns, but others are "noun markers" that modify nouns only.

* descriptive words

  EXAMPLES:
  beautiful music, *blue* sky, *large* room

* articles

  EXAMPLES:
  a table, *an* artichoke, *the* end

* numbers

  EXAMPLES:
  six hours, *200* pages

* possessive nouns and pronouns

EXAMPLES:

my house, *his* bike, *Anne's* mother

* other pronouns, when they come before a noun

EXAMPLES:

Which sweater did *each* girl choose—*this* one or *that* one?

* noun adjectives: These are nouns used to describe other nouns. Almost any noun can become a noun adjective when you put it before another noun.

EXAMPLES:

guitar solo (tells what kind of solo)

car salesman (tells what kind of salesman)

pet spider (tells what kind of spider)

* proper adjectives: These are adjectives made from proper nouns. They begin with a capital letter, just like the nouns they are made from.

EXAMPLES:

proper noun: France

proper adjective: *French* bread

proper noun: Ireland

proper adjective: *Irish* jig

* verbals: Some verb forms can be used as descriptive words.

EXAMPLES:

a *forgotten* diary   the *defeated* team

running water   a *spinning* top

(NOTE: For more information on verbals, see pps. 91–98.)

*adjective phrases and clauses: These are groups of words that act together as a single adjective.

EXAMPLES:

adjective phrase:
The boy *at the next table* is David.
(tells which boy)

adjective clause:
The dress *that she bought* is too small.
(tells which dress)

NOTE: For more information, see "Participial Phrases," p. 92; "Infinitives," p. 96; "Adjective Phrase or Adverb Phrase?" p. 119; and "Adjective Clauses," p. 137.

WHERE TO LOOK FOR ADJECTIVES

Adjectives are usually found right before a noun, right after a noun, or after a linking verb.

NOTE: Some adjectives, such as articles, numbers, and possessive adjectives, usually come before the noun.

EXAMPLES:

before a noun:
This *good-looking, economical* car is your best bet.

after a noun:
This car, *good-looking* and *economical*, is your best bet.

after a linking verb:
This car is *good-looking* and *economical*.

PUNCTUATION POINTERS:
Adjectives

* When to use a comma

When two or more adjectives of equal importance come before a noun, separate them with commas. How can you tell if the adjectives are of equal importance? If you can change the order or put *and* between them, *use commas*. Do not use a comma between the last adjective and the noun.

EXAMPLES:

no comma
She wore blue wool pants.
(You could not say *wool blue pants* or *blue and wool pants*.)

comma
The clapping, cheering crowd rose to their feet.
(You could say *cheering, clapping crowd* or *clapping and cheering crowd*.)

* When to use a hyphen

Many two-word adjectives are hyphenated, especially when they come before a noun. The hyphen shows that the two words belong together and should be read as one.

EXAMPLES:

Who is that *well-dressed* stranger?
Give me twenty-five dollar bills. ($25)
Give me twenty five-dollar bills. ($100)

ADVERBS

An *adverb* modifies—tells more about—a verb, adjective, or another adverb. It tells *how, when, where,* or *to what extent*.

ADVERBS THAT TELL *HOW*

These adverbs usually modify verbs. They are usually formed by adding *ly* to an adjective.

EXAMPLES:

adjective:
The room was *quiet*.

adverb:
I *quietly* entered the room.
(entered how?)

adjective:
A *threatening* dog stood in our path.

adverb:
It growled *threateningly*.

NOTE: Some words that end in -*ly* are not adverbs. They are adjectives.

EXAMPLES:

a *deadly* chemical, a *friendly* person

NOTE: some adverbs that end in -*ly* tell *when*:

EXAMPLE:

immediately

FORMING ADVERBS WITH -*LY*

* When the adjective ends in *l*, the adverb has a double *l*:
    careful-carefully
    grateful-gratefully

* When the adjective ends in *ic*, add *ally*:
  artistic-artistically   basic-basically

* When the adjective ends in *y*, change the *y* to *i* before adding *ly*:
  noisy-noisily   sleepy-sleepily

* When the adjective ends in *ble*, drop the *e* before adding *ly*:
  invisible-invisibly   lovable-lovably

ADVERBS THAT TELL *WHEN*

These adverbs modify verbs. Some of them tell *how often* or *how long*.

EXAMPLES:

when?
I went to the movies *yesterday*.

how often?
She *sometimes* goes with me.

how long?
The last movie we saw seemed to last *forever*.

NOTE: Some WHEN adverbs can also be nouns See "Adverb or Noun?" p. 108.)

NUMBER ADVERBS

The "number adverbs" tell *in what order* or *how many times*.

EXAMPLES:

in what order?   We saw the cartoons *first*.

how many times?   We saw that movie *twice*.

ADVERBS THAT TELL *WHERE*

These adverbs modify verbs. They tell *in what location* or *in what direction*.

EXAMPLES:

Jill went *upstairs*.

Turn *left*.

She went *away*, and we went *inside*.

NOTE: Some WHERE adverbs can also be prepositions. See "Preposition or Adverb?" p. 119.

NOTE: Some WHERE adverbs can also be nouns. See "Adverb or Noun?" p. 108.

ADVERBS THAT TELL *TO WHAT EXTENT*

These adverbs usually modify adjectives or other adverbs. When they do, they are called *intensifiers*. Here is a list of the most common ones. The intensifiers are in italics.

EXAMPLES:

very tired	*quite* sorry
almost gladly	*more* attractive
extremely windy	*rather* reluctantly
too suddenly	*somewhat* carelessly
less impatient	

QUESTION ADVERBS

The words *how, when, where,* and *why* are adverbs when they are used to ask questions.

EXAMPLES:

When are you going?

How did you know?

SENTENCE ADVERBS

These adverbs tell more about a whole sentence rather than about any particular word.

EXAMPLES:

Unfortunately, we won't be able to go.

Actually, we have a book report due on Monday.

She found out, *apparently*, by asking Dot.

NEGATIVE ADVERBS

The word *not* and the contraction *n't* are adverbs. Other common negative adverbs are *hardly, scarcely, barely*, and *never*. See "How to Avoid Double Negatives," p. 107.

ADVERB PHRASES AND CLAUSES

Groups of words often work together as a single adverb.

EXAMPLES:

adverb phrases:

how long?   where?   why?
We drove *for three hours/on Route 9/to reach your house.*

adverb clauses:

When the bell rang, I ran to the door *because I had to talk to Steve.*

NOTE: For more information, see "Adjective Phrase or Adverb Phrase?" p. 119; "Infinitives," p. 96; and "Adverb Clauses," p. 132.

HOW TO AVOID DOUBLE NEGATIVES

Don't use two negative words in close relationship with each other. Negative words include *not*, the contraction *n't*, *never*, *nothing*, *nobody*, *nowhere*, *no one*, *none*, *hardly*, *scarcely*, *barely*.

EXAMPLES:

Don't say:	She could*n't* *hardly* see.
Say:	She *could hardly* see.
Don't say:	We *never* go *nowhere*.
Say:	We *never* go *anywhere*.
Don't say:	I do*n't* see *nothing* wrong with it.
Say:	I do*n't* see *anything* wrong with it.
Or say:	I see *nothing* wrong with it.
Don't say:	*Hardly nobody* showed up.
Say:	*Hardly anybody* showed up.

WHERE TO LOOK FOR ADVERBS

Adverbs can appear almost anywhere in a sentence. Sometimes it doesn't matter where you put an adverb.

EXAMPLES:

Suddenly, the sun appeared.

The sun *suddenly* appeared.

The sun appeared *suddenly*.

Sometimes it *does* matter where you put an adverb. The location of the adverb can change the meaning of the sentence. This happens most often with the adverbs *only*, *just*, *not*, and *never*.

EXAMPLES:

Only he gave me flowers yesterday.
(no one else gave)

He gave *only* me flowers yesterday.
(he gave no one else)

He gave me *only* flowers yesterday.
(that's all he gave)

He gave me flowers *only* yesterday.
(just yesterday)

He *just* wasn't a good athlete.
(He wasn't a good athlete.)

He wasn't *just* a good athlete.
(He was a good athlete and more.)

ADVERB OR NOUN?

Some words can be either adverbs or nouns, depending on how they are used in a sentence. When they modify a verb, they are adverbs. When they are used as subjects, direct objects, objects of the preposition, etc., they are nouns.

EXAMPLES:

adverbs:
She is going *home today*.

noun—subject
Today is the first day of the rest of your life.

noun—subject
Her *home* is in Colorado.

WHEN TO USE AN ADJECTIVE AND WHEN TO USE AN ADVERB

Many people have trouble deciding when to use an ajdective and when to use an adverb.

Here are some clues to help you choose the right modifier.

PROBLEM:

We worked steady/steadily on the car until six o'clock.

(adj.) steady   *(adv.)* steadily

CLUES:

* Does the sentence need a word to tell *what kind, how many,* or *which one* about a noun? If so, choose the adjective form.

* Does the sentence need a word to tell *how, when,* or *where* about a verb? Does it need a word to strengthen the meaning of an adjective or adverb? In either case, choose the adverb form.

SOLUTION:

The sentence above needs an *adverb* to tell *how* we worked. The correct choice is *steadily*.

PROBLEMS:

a. I felt sad/sadly.

b. I felt the snake careful/carefully.

c. I tasted the cookies unwilling/unwillingly.

d. The cookies tasted strange/strangely.

CLUES:

Use an adjective after a linking verb, and use an adverb after an action verb. The problem is that some verbs can be *either* linking verbs or action verbs (see p. 79). How can you tell which is which? Ask yourself these questions:

*In which sentences does the subject actually *do* something? These sentences need an adverb to tell *how* an action is done.

*In which sentences is the subject being described? These sentences need an adjective.

SOLUTIONS:

a. The subject did not perform the action of feeling (touching) anything. The subject is merely being described. The correct choice is *sad*.

b. The verb *felt* tells what the subject *did*. The sentence needs an *adverb* to tell *how* the action was done. The correct choice is *carefully*.

c. Did the subject *I* do something? Yes. The sentence needs an *adverb* to tell *how* the action was done. *Unwillingly* is the right choice.

d. Did the cookies actually taste something? No. The sentence needs an adjective to describe the cookies. *Strange* is the right choice.

CONFUSING ADJECTIVE/ ADVERB PAIRS

Here are some adjective-adverb pairs that are often misused.

REMEMBER: Use the adjective form to modify a noun or pronoun. Use the adverb form to modify a verb, adjective, or another adverb.

ADJECTIVES	ADVERBS
real	really
good	well (when it tells how an action is done)

well (when it means *not sick*)	—
bad	badly
sure	surely
awful	awfully
easy	easily

USAGE SAMPLES: The best way to start using these words correctly is to repeat the correct usages until they start "sounding right" to you. Here are some sample sentences that can help you:

This is a *real* diamond.
(adj.—modifies noun, *diamond*)

It is *really* valuable.
(adv.—modifies adj., *valuable*)

I feel *good*.
(means happy, opposite of bad, adj. describing *I*)

I feel *well*.
(means healthy, opposite of sick, adj. describing *I*)

I feel *bad*.

I have a *bad* cold.

She draws *well*.

I slept *well*.

Stir it *well*.

She reacted *badly*.

It hurt *badly*.

I am *sure*.

I am *surely* sorry.

It was *awful*.

It was *awfully* long.

It was an *easy* game.
We won *easily*.

DOUBLE-DUTY MODIFIERS

A few words can be used either as adjectives or as adverbs.

EXAMPLES:

	ADJECTIVE	ADVERB
deep	a deep river	went deep (or deeply) into the cave
early	an early train	They came early.
fast	a fast ride	She drove fast.
hard	a hard choice	He hit the ball hard.
high	The price was high.	The plane flew high.
late	a late start	started late
long	a long journey	We didn't stay long.
low	a low sound	She whispered low.
near	We were near the restaurant.	He stood near.
slow	a slow boat	walked slow (or slowly)
straight	a straight road	The arrow flew straight.

NOTE: Some of these words also have *ly* forms that can be used in their place.

EXAMPLES:

He went slow.   He went slowly.

Slowly is the preferred form in a longer sentence: We traveled *slowly* down the long, winding road.

NOTE: Sometimes the *ly* form has a different meaning.

EXAMPLES:

The movie started *late*.

Lately, we have been seeing more movies.

She slammed the door *hard*.

It *hardly* matters.

The elephant stood so *near* we could touch it.

I *nearly* fainted.

MAKING COMPARISONS WITH ADJECTIVES AND ADVERBS

Most adjectives and adverbs have three forms: the *positive*, the *comparative*, and the *superlative*.

* The *positive* is the regular form of the adjective or adverb.
* The *comparative* is formed with *-er* or *more*. It is used to compare two items.
* The *superlative* is formed with *-est* or *most*. It is used to compare three or more items.

	POSITIVE	COMPARATIVE	SUPERLATIVE
Adjectives:	tame	tamer	tamest
	simple	simpler	simplest
	helpful	more helpful	most helpful
	romantic	more romantic	most romantic

Adverbs:	soon	sooner	soonest
	quickly	more quickly	most quickly

RULES FOR MAKING COMPARISONS

* Use the comparative to compare two items and the superlative to compare three or more.

EXAMPLES:

This dictionary is the *more helpful* of the two.

He is the *taller* of the two boys.

I am the *shortest* person in the class.

* Use *-er* and *-est* for one syllable words.

EXAMPLES:

ripe-riper-ripest

near-nearer-nearest

* Use *more* and *most* for words with three or more syllables.

EXAMPLE:

dangerous, more dangerous, most dangerous

* Some two-syllable words always take *-er* and *-est*. Some always take *more* and *most*. And some can use either method. The only way to be sure is to consult a good dictionary.

EXAMPLES:

silly-sillier-silliest

hopeful-more hopeful-most hopeful

sorry-sorrier-sorriest

sorry-more sorry-most sorry

114

* Adverbs that end in *ly* are always compared with *more* and *most*.

EXAMPLES:

quickly-more quickly-most quickly

strictly-more strictly-most strictly

* Don't use double comparisons
  Don't use both *-er* and *more* or both *-est* and *most* in the same comparison.

EXAMPLES:

Don't say:	Is Steve Martin more funnier than Chevy Chase?
Say:	Is Steve Martin funnier than Chevy Chase?
Or say:	Is Steve Martin more funny than Chevy Chase?

* Less and least
  The opposite of *-er* and *more* is *less*.
  The opposite of *-est* and *most* is *least*.

EXAMPLES:

The stain seems *less* noticeable now.

We went swimming *less* often last summer.

He is the *least* friendly person I know.

* Any other/anyone else
  When comparing an individual with other members of a group that he or she belongs to, use the expressions *any other* or *anyone else*.

EXAMPLES:

| Don't say: | Bob runs faster than any player on the team. (This is |

	correct only if Bob himself is *not* on the team.)
Say:	Bob runs faster than *any other* player on the team.
Or say:	Bob runs faster than *anyone else* on the team.

NOTE: Without the words *other* or *else*, the sentences would mean either that Bob himself wasn't on the team or that he was faster than any player, including himself.

* Words beyond compare
Some adjectives express qualities that cannot be compared. For example, one thing cannot be "more perfect" than another. Either something is perfect or it is not. Other examples include: *square, round, unique, endless,* and *impossible.* If you want to compare things that are *almost* round, impossible, etc., you can say that one thing is *more nearly* round, or the *most nearly* impossible, etc.

* Compared to what?
Make sure that you clearly express what items you are actually comparing.

EXAMPLE:

Don't say:	The dances at North High are better than South High. (compares dances to a school)
Say:	The dances at North High are better than *those* at South High.

IRREGULAR COMPARISONS

A few adjectives and adverbs have special comparative and superlative forms that have to be memorized. In some cases, an adjective and an adverb will share the same comparative and superlative forms.

	COMPARATIVE	SUPERLATIVE
little	less	least
good	better	best
well	better	best
bad	worse	worst
badly	worse	worst
many	more	most
much	more	most
far (distance)	farther	farthest
far (degree)	further	furthest

EXAMPLES:

I feel *bad* now that I know how *badly* the dog was treated.

I feel *worse* now that I know that the dog was treated even *worse* than I had thought.

PREPOSITIONS

A *preposition* shows the relationship between the noun or pronoun that follows it and some other word in the sentence.

* The noun or pronoun that follows the preposition is called the *object of the preposition*.
* The preposition + its object is called a *prepositional phrase*.
* Notice how changing the preposition in the sen-

tence below changes the relationship between the verb *swam* and the object of the preposition, *sharks*.

	prepositional phrase	
	prepositions	object
Jack swam —	above ———————	the sharks.
	around	
	with	
	between	
	like	
	in spite of	
	toward	
	because of	
	past	

COMMON PREPOSITIONS

about	between	in	through-
above	beyond	into	out
across	but	inside	to
after	(meaning	like	toward
against	except)	of	under
along	by	off	under-
among	concerning	on	neath
around	despite	onto	until
at	down	out	unto
before	during	outside	up
behind	except	over	upon
below	for	past	with
beneath	from	regarding	within
beside		since	without
besides		through	

COMPOUND PREPOSITIONS

A *compound preposition* is two or more words that act together to express one relationship. Each group of words is treated as one preposition.

according to	because of	instead of
along with	by way of	on account of
apart from	except for	on top of
as far as	in regard to	out of
aside from	in addition to	together with
as to	in spite of	

PREPOSITION OR ADVERB?

Many of the words in the "Common Prepositions" chart on p. 118 can be either prepositions or adverbs. When they are followed by a noun or pronoun, they are prepositions. When they are not followed by a noun or a pronoun, they are adverbs.

EXAMPLES:

I went *outside*. (adverb)

The ball flew *outside* the stadium. (preposition)

I fell *down*. (adverb)

She went *down* the stairs slowly. (preposition)

ADJECTIVE PHRASE or ADVERB PHRASE?

Prepositional phrases are *always* modifiers. They can be either *adjective phrases* or *adverb phrases*, depending on the words they modify.

* An *adjective phrase* modifies a noun or pronoun.

EXAMPLES:

The girl *behind me* coughed.

The title *of the story* is "In Another Country."

* An **adverb phrase** modifies a verb, an adjective, or another adverb.

EXAMPLES:

We walked *in the rain*.

I looked *through the window*.

DANGER: DANGLING MODIFIERS!

Modifiers of all kinds are a little like clinging vines. They tend to attach themselves to the nearest word that can be modified, sometimes with hilarious results. Always make sure that the modifiers you use are attaching themselves to the words you *want* them to modify.

EXAMPLES:

Don't say: *Weak and hungry*, the rescue ship picked up the castaways.

(Was the rescue ship weak and hungry?)

Say: *Weak and hungry*, the castaways were picked up by the rescue ship.

Or say: The *weak and hungry* castaways were picked up by the rescue ship.

Don't say: *Shattering into a thousand pieces*, Angie screamed as she dropped the precious vase.

(Unless Angie shattered into a thousand pieces, this sentence needs help.)

Say:	As the precious vase fell and *shattered into a thousand pieces,* Angie screamed.
Don't say:	*With their razor-sharp teeth and lightning-quick jaws,* many visitors to the aquarium are drawn to the sharks. (Unless the visitors are the dangerous ones!)
Say:	*With their razor-sharp teeth and lightning-quick jaws,* the sharks are a big attraction to many aquarium visitors.
Don't say:	*When listening to loud music on the stereo,* my entire house shakes.
Say:	*When I'm listening to loud music on the stereo, my entire house shakes.*

You get the idea, right? Just remember that it's harder to catch yourself in the act of writing a dangling modifier than it is to recognize one that somebody else has already written.

MAKING CONNECTIONS:

How to Use Conjunctions and Clauses to Build Sentences

CONJUNCTIONS MAKE CONNECTIONS

Conjunctions connect words or groups of words.

* *Coordinating conjunctions* connect sentence parts of equal importance. They are used to connect words to words, phrases to phrases, and clauses to other clauses of equal importance.

EXAMPLES:

and, but, or, nor
(used to connect words, phrases, or clauses)

for, so, yet
(used to connect clauses only)

plus
(used to connect words or phrases only)

* *Correlative conjunctions* are coordinating conjunctions that work in pairs. Like other coordinating conjunctions, they connect words, phrases, or clauses of equal importance.

EXAMPLES:

both . . . and   not only . . . but also

neither . . . nor   either . . . or

* *Subordinating conjunctions* are used only to connect a *dependent clause* to an *independent clause*. (See p. 132.)

EXAMPLES:

until, although, because, after, etc.

CLAUSES ARE CONNECT-ABLE

A *clause* is any group of words that has a subject and a predicate. There are two different kinds:

* An *independent clause* is one that makes sense all by itself. It can stand alone as a sentence *or* be connected to other clauses. An independent clause is sometimes called a *main clause*.

* A *dependent clause* is one that cannot stand alone. It *must* be joined to an independent clause to make sense. A dependent clause is sometimes called a *subordinate clause*. For more information, see "Adverb Clauses," p. 132; "Adjective Clauses," p. 137; and "Noun Clauses," p. 141.

MAKING CONNECTIONS:
The Simple Sentence

A *simple sentence* consists of one *independent* clause (and no dependent clauses). In a simple sentence, conjunctions are used only to join words to words and phrases to phrases. A simple sentence may sometimes look long and complicated when it has compound parts or many modifiers. But as long as it contains just one clause, it is still a simple sentence. All of the examples below are simple sentences.

EXAMPLES:

He washed the dishes.

He and I washed the dishes.
(simple sentence with compound subject)

He washed the dishes and put them away.
(simple sentence with compound verb)

He and I washed the dishes and put them away.
(simple sentence with compound subject and compound verb. Since both subjects *share* the same verbs there is only one clause.)

He and I washed the dishes very carefully and put them away in the cupboard above the sink.
(simple sentence with compound subject and compound verb + modifiers.)

WRITING TIPS:
Simple Sentence Connections

NOTE: You should always use the kind of sentence that expresses your ideas most clearly. Long sentences are not necessarily better than short sentences. Sometimes they will express your ideas more clearly and sometimes they won't. The important thing is to use a *variety* of sentence patterns to make your writing more interesting. For more ideas on sentence connections, see the other writing tips in this chapter.

* Use compound subjects and verbs sometimes.

Using compound subjects and compound verbs is one way you can avoid writing too many short sentences in a row. Use this technique sometimes to add variety to your writing.

EXAMPLES:

two short sentences:

I went to Jane's for the weekend. I had a good time.

one sentence with compound verb:

I went to Jane's for the weekend and had a good time.

two short sentences:

Harry has a hard time with Spanish. So does Ann.

one sentence with compound subject:

Harry and Ann have a hard time with Spanish.

* Connect similar words and phrases.

Make sure that the words and phrases you connect are similar (a noun and a noun, an adjective and an adjective, a prepositional phrase and a prepositional phrase, an -*ing* phrase and an -*ing* phrase, etc.

EXAMPLES:

Don't say: My goals for this summer are *finding* a job and *to save* money.

Say: My goals for this summer are *finding* a job and *saving* money.

125

Or say:	My goals for this summer are *to find* a job and *to save* money.
Don't say:	Magic Johnson is famous for his *shooting, rebounding,* and *the way* he handles the ball.
Say:	Magic Johnson is famous for his *shooting, rebounding,* and fantastic *ball-handling*.
Or say:	Magic Johnson is famous for the way he *shoots, rebounds,* and *handles* the ball.

NOTE: A similar rule applies to comparisons using *than* and *as*.

EXAMPLES:

Don't say:	It's better *to go* early than *waiting* until after lunch.
Say:	It's better *to go* early than *to wait* until after lunch.
Or say:	*Going early* is a better idea than *waiting* until after lunch.

* Use pairs of conjunctions correctly.
When using conjunctions that work in pairs, be sure to put them right before the words they connect.

EXAMPLE:

Don't say:	I either saw that movie with you or Jeffrey.
Say:	I saw that movie with either you or Jeffrey.

MAKING CONNECTIONS:
THE COMPOUND SENTENCE

A *compound sentence* consists of two or more *independent* clauses (clauses that can stand alone as sentences). Usually, the clauses are connected by a *comma* + a *coordinating conjunction*.

EXAMPLES:

two sentences:

I asked Martin to turn down the volume.

He didn't pay any attention to me.

one compound sentence:

I asked Martin to turn down the volume, *but* he didn't pay any attention to me.

three sentences:

Molly bought the refreshments.

Tim provided the music.

I volunteered our basement for the party.

one compound sentence:

Molly bought the refreshments, Tim provided the music, *and* I volunteered our basement for the party.

PUNCTUATION POINTERS:
Ways to Connect Independent Clauses

* You can connect independent clauses with a *comma* + a *coordinating conjunction*.

EXAMPLE:

I asked her to help me plan the party, *and* she said she would be glad to help out.

NOTE: Sometimes, when the clauses are short, you don't need to use a comma.

EXAMPLE:

I asked her to help and she did.

But sometimes, even when the clauses are short, you should still use a comma to avoid confusion.

EXAMPLE:

I voted for Linda, and Susan did likewise.

* You can connect independent clauses with a *comma* + a pair of *correlative conjunctions*.

EXAMPLE:

Not only did my feet hurt, *but also* my back ached.

* You can connect independent clauses with a *semicolon* + a *coordinate adverb*. Coordinating adverbs include: *therefore, accordingly, also, besides, hence, however, likewise, moreover, indeed, otherwise, consequently, nonetheless, then,* and *thus*. When the coordinating adverb is the first word in the second clause, it is always followed by a comma. When it appears in other positions, it may or may not be set off by commas.

EXAMPLES:

I know this sounds incredible; *however*, it is a true story.

I know this sound incredible; it is, *however*, a true story.

I know this sounds incredible; it is a true story, *however*.

* You can connect independent clauses with a *semicolon* alone.

EXAMPLE:

I was there to participate; Jane was there to watch.

* DO NOT connect two independent clauses with just a comma. If you do, you'll have a run-on sentence.

Don't write:	Crossword puzzles are fun, they help you learn about words.
Write:	Crossword puzzles are fun, and they help you learn about words.
Or:	Not only are crossword puzzles fun, but also they help you learn about words.
Or:	Crossword puzzles are fun; in addition, they help you learn about words.
Or:	Crossword puzzles are fun. They also help you learn about words.

**PUNCTUATION POINTER:
Compound Sentence or Compound
Verb? When to Use a Comma**

Use a comma before a coordinating conjunction in a compound sentence. DO NOT ordinarily use a comma before a conjunction that joins two verbs in a simple sentence.

EXAMPLES:

The principal announced the results of the contest, and everyone in our homeroom cheered.

(Use a comma because this is a compound sentence. There is an independent clause on either side of the conjunction.)

The principal announced the results of the contest and asked everyone to congratulate the winners.

(Don't use a comma. This is a simple sentence with a compound verb. The conjunction joins two verbs with the same subject.)

WRITING TIP:
Compound Sentence Connections

* Don't connect two sentences unless there is a natural relationship between them.

EXAMPLES:
connection between ideas:
I saw Leslie at the movie, and I went out with her afterward.

no connection:
I saw Leslie at the movie, and I bought some popcorn.

* Choose the conjunction or coordinating adverb that best expresses the connection you want to make between two ideas. The chart below shows how you can use different words to suggest different connections.

TO EXPRESS RELATED IDEAS: Use *and, moreover, indeed, also, besides, furthermore, in addition,* or *likewise.*

TO SHOW THAT ONE THING RESULTS FROM ANOTHER: Use *so, consequently, therefore, thus,* or *accordingly.*

TO EXPRESS A CHOICE OR A DIFFER-
ENCE: Use *or* or *otherwise*.

TO EXPRESS A CONTRAST: Use *but*, *however*, *still*, *nevertheless*, or *nonetheless*.

EXAMPLES:

Don't say:	The pizza was good, and we couldn't finish it.
Say:	The pizza was good, but we couldn't finish it.
Or say:	The pizza was good; never-theless, we couldn't finish it.
Don't say:	We have to clean up this mess, and we won't be al-lowed to bake cookies again.
Say:	We have to clean up this mess, or we won't be al-lowed to bake cookies again.
Or say:	We have to clean up this mess; otherwise, we won't be allowed to bake cookies again.

MAKING CONNECTIONS:
The Complex Sentence

A *complex sentence* consists of one *independent clause* + at least one *dependent clause*

* The *independent clause* is the one that can stand alone as a sentence. It is often called the *main clause* because it expresses the main idea of the sentence.

* The *dependent clause* is also called a *subordinate clause*. It begins with a word called a *subordinator*

(for example: *until, that, who, although*). The subordinator is the word that makes the clause dependent on the main clause. Without the subordinator, the dependent clause would make sense by itself and be an independent clause.

EXAMPLE:

dependent clause: until you left

independent clause: You left.

* There are three kinds of dependent clauses: *adverb clauses, adjective clauses,* and *noun clauses.*

ADVERB CLAUSES

An *adverb clause* is a dependent clause that modifies—tells more about—a verb, an adjective, or another adverb. It tells *how, when, where, why, to what extent,* or *under what conditions.* An adverb clause begins with a *subordinating conjunction.*

SUBORDINATING CONJUNCTIONS

If you learn to recognize the subordinating conjunctions, you'll be able to spot adverb clauses more easily. Here is a list of the most common ones:

after	before	until
although	if	when
as	since	whenever
as if	so that	where
as long as	than	wherever
as soon as	though	whether
as though	unless	while
because		

> NOTE: Some of the words on this list can also be adverbs and prepositions. To be subordinating conjunctions, they must be followed by a subject and a verb.

Adverb Clauses: Examples

Adverb clause telling HOW:
He acted *as if he already knew*.

Adverb clause telling WHERE:
Move your chair *wherever you'd like*.

Adverb clause telling WHY:
She's staying after school *because Ms. Armstrong asked her*.

Adverb clause telling WHEN:
Before you go, would you do me a favor?

Adverb clause telling TO WHAT EXTENT
or HOW MUCH:
It snowed more *than the weatherman predicted*.

Adverb clause telling UNDER WHAT CONDITIONS:
If I tell you a secret, will you promise not to repeat it?

NOTE: Just like single-word adverbs, adverb clauses can occur almost anywhere in a sentence.

EXAMPLES:
If I can, I'll come five minutes early.
I'll come five minutes early *if I can*.

NOTE: An *elliptical* adverb clause is one in which the subject and/or verb are understood, but not expressed.

EXAMPLES:
I have been here longer *than you* (have been here).
I love you more today *than* (I did) *yesterday*.

133

WRITING TIPS:
Adverb Clauses

* A sentence that connects two thoughts with an adverb clause can sometimes help you express your ideas more clearly than two short sentences can. Adverb clauses can also help you avoid stringing our your thoughts with *and, so,* and *but.* Remember: Your goal is to use a wide variety of sentence patterns to make your writing more interesting.

EXAMPLES:

four simple sentences:

We arrived at the amusement park.

Sue wanted to ride the Wildcat right away.

I wasn't so sure. I eventually agreed.

two compound sentences:

We arrived at the amusement park, and Sue wanted to ride the Wildcat right away. I wasn't so sure, but I eventually agreed.

one complex sentence + one compound sentence

When we arrived at the amusement park, Sue wanted to ride the Wildcat right away. I wasn't so sure, but I eventually agreed.

* Choose the subordinating conjunction that best expresses the connection you want to make between two ideas. One little word can sometimes make a big difference.

I wanted to go out for pizza after the show started at eight o'clock.

before
unless
because
although

134

* Never let an adverb clause "hang loose" in your writing, or you'll have a sentence fragment. REMEMBER: Adverb clauses cannot stand alone. They must be joined to an independent clause.

EXAMPLES:

Don't write: Amy helped me clean my room. Because I couldn't handle the job alone.

(The first group of words that ends with a period is a sentence. The second group is not, because the subordinating word *because* makes it dependent on the first sentence.)

Write: Amy helped me clean my room because I couldn't handle the job alone.

PUNCTUATION POINTERS:
Adverb Clauses

* Always use a comma after an adverb clause that begins a sentence.

EXAMPLE:

When I go away, I'll get you a present.

* Adverb clauses that come in the middle of the sentence are interrupters. Set them off with commas.

EXAMPLE:

Tell me, if you don't mind, why you waited so long.

* In most cases DO NOT use a comma before an adverb clause that comes at the end of a sentence. Here are some exceptions:

  * Use a comma if the clause supplies extra information, but not if it supplies essential information.

  EXAMPLES:

  essential: no comma

  Let's stop *as soon as we see a restaurant*.

  extra: use comma

  Let's go to Burger Delight at six o'clock, when everyone else will be there.

  * Use a comma if the clause begins with *though* or *although*.

  EXAMPLES:

  I'm always five minutes late, although I try to be on time.

  * Use a comma when the clause begins with *as* or *since* (only when they mean *because*).

  EXAMPLES:

  I'm doing extra work now, since I won't be here next semester. (use comma)

  I'm doing extra work now, as I won't be here next semester.
  (use comma)

  I've been taking ballet lessons since the fourth grade.
  (no comma)

  I'm taking shop as an elective.
  (no comma)

  * Use a comma if the clause begins with *while* (only when it means *but*).

ADJECTIVE CLAUSES

An *adjective clause* is a dependent clause that
modifies—tells more about—a noun or pronoun.
It usually tells *which one* or *what kind*. An adjective
clause usually begins with a *relative pronoun*. The
relative pronoun relates the clause to a noun or
pronoun in the main clause.

RELATIVE PRONOUNS

that
which
who, whom, whose
whoever, whomever
which

Adjective Clauses: Examples

The show <u>that ended at ten o'clock</u> was terrible.
The waitress <u>who served us</u> was Gail's sister.
The guests <u>whom I invited</u> are all showing up.
This dress, <u>which I bought on sale</u>, is my favorite.

NOTE: The relative pronoun in each clause relates
back to a noun or pronoun in the main clause. It
also serves as a subject or object within the clause
itself.

NOTE: Some adjective clauses are introduced by adverbs such as *where, why, after, when,* and *before.* Even though these clauses begin with adverbs, they are still adjective clauses as long as they tell more about a noun or pronoun in the main clause.

EXAMPLES:

The lake *where we swim* is in the mountains.
(tells which lake)
The night *before I left* I almost decided to stay home.
(tells which night)

USAGE TIPS:
who/that/which/who/whom

* Who/which/that

  Use *who* to refer to people (and to those special animals who seem to have as much personality as people!).

  Use *which* to refer to animals and things only, never to people.

  Use *that* to refer to people, things, or animals.

* Who/whom

  Remember that *who* is used as a subject and *whom* is used as an object. When deciding which word to use in a clause, consider only the clause itself. Ignore any words outside the clause. If the clause needs a subject, use *who*. If the clause needs an object, use *whom*.

  EXAMPLES:

  My great-aunt, [whom I have never met,] is coming to visit

  My great-aunt, [who lives in Smithville,] is coming to visit.

NOTE: For more help with *who* and *whom*, see pp. 36–38 and p. 144.

WRITING TIPS:
Adjective Clauses

* Using adjective clauses is another way to add variety to your writing and express your ideas more clearly.

EXAMPLES:

Okay: The Warriors are our biggest competitors, and they have won twelve games straight. Their best player is out with a knee injury but will be back next week. His future performance could determine the championships. We will watch it closely.

Better: The Warriors, *who have won twelve games straight*, are our biggest competitors. Their best player is out with a knee injury but will be back next week. His future performance, *which we will watch closely*, could determine the championships.

* When connecting two ideas in a sentence with an adjective clause, be sure to put the main idea in the main clause and the less important idea in the adjective clause. For example, take one of the sentences from the example above:

The Warriors, *who have won twelve games straight*, are our biggest competitors.

This sentence emphasizes the fact that the Warriors are our competitors. If you want to emphasize the winning streak, write it this way:

The Warriors, *who are our competitors*, have won twelve games straight.

PUNCTUATION POINTERS:
Use Commas to Set Off
Extra Information

* Some adjective clauses supply *essential* information. They narrow down the meaning of the noun they modify by telling *which one*. Without these clauses, the essential meaning of the sentence would be lost. *Do not use commas with essential clauses*.

EXAMPLE:

The singer *whom I admire most* is Linda Ronstadt.

(Try reading this sentence without the clause. You'll see that the information it supplies is essential. Without it, the meaning of the sentence is lost.)

* Other adjective clauses *interrupt* the flow of the sentence by supplying *extra, descriptive* information that is *not essential* to the meaning of the sentence. *Use commas with these clauses* to show that the reader should pause for an interruption.

EXAMPLE:

The lead singer, *who has been with the band for seven years*, always wears a flower in her hair.

(The clause in this sentence does *not* supply essential information. It interrupts the main message of the sentence to give *extra* information about the lead singer. Commas are used to show that it interrupts the sentence.

NOTE: The same rules apply to adjective phrases and to appositive nouns. *Extra* information is set off by commas. *Essential* information is not.

EXAMPLES:

ESSENTIAL: The player *now warming up* is George Brett.

(The phrase gives essential information about which player you are talking about; no commas.)

EXTRA: George Brett, *now warming up,* is one of the best hitters in the League.

(The phrase now supplies extra information that interrupts the main message of the sentence; use commas.)

ESSENTIAL: My brother Jeffrey really knows how to annoy me.

(This is how you would write the sentence if you had more than one brother. In that case, the word *Jeffrey* would be essential to indicate which brother you meant; no commas.)

EXTRA: My brother, Jeffrey, really knows how to annoy me.

(This is how you would write the sentence if you had only one brother. In that case, the word *Jeffrey* would be extra information. It would not be necessary to clarify which brother you meant; use commas.)

NOUN CLAUSES

A *noun clause* is a dependent clause that does the job of a noun. That is, it can be a *subject, direct object, object of the preposition,* or *predicate nominative.*

WORDS THAT INTRODUCE NOUN CLAUSES

who	whether
whoever	when
whom	where
whomever	why
whose	how
whosever	if
which	that
whichever	
what	
whatever	

Noun Clauses: Examples

noun as subject:
Pete is in trouble.

noun clause as subject:
Whoever left the ice cream out is in trouble.

noun as predicate nominative:
The problem is *space*.

noun clause as predicate nominative:
The problem is *that we can't fit fifty teenagers into a tiny basement*.

noun as direct object:
Tell me *the secret*.

noun clause as direct object:
Tell me *when we are leaving*.
whether I should go.
what she said.
if he wants to go.

noun as object of the preposition:
Give the invitation to *Judy*.

noun clause as object of the preposition:
Give the invitation to *whoever answers the door*.
Give the invitation to *whomever you wish*.

What Kind of Clause Is It? How to tell

Many of the words that introduce noun clauses can also introduce adjective or adverb clauses. You usually have to take a look at the whole clause to see whether it is acting as a noun or a modifier.

EXAMPLES:
Find out *when she's coming to visit*.

(This clause answers the question *find out what*? It is acting as a direct object. You could substitute a noun such as "the answer" in its place. Therefore, it is a noun clause.)

When she comes to visit, we'll all get together.

(This clause simply tells when. It is an adverb clause.)

That we actually saw a UFO has not been proved.

(This clause is acting as the subject of the sentence. It must be a noun clause.)

The object *that we saw* may have been something very ordinary.

(*That we saw* tells which object. It is an adjective clause.)

WRITING TIPS:
Using Noun Clauses

Using noun clauses is yet another way to connect two ideas in one sentence.

EXAMPLES:

two sentences:
The game was all over.
We knew it.

one sentence with noun clause:
We knew *that the game was all over*.

two sentences:
Someone will get all the right answers.
Give this prize to that person.

one sentence with noun clause:
Give this prize to *whoever gets all the right answers*.

USAGE TIP:
who/whom

Who and *whoever* are used as subjects of a noun clause. *Whom* and *whomever* are used as objects. When choosing between them in a clause, *ignore the words outside the clause—especially prepositions.* Consider only how the pronoun is used within the clause. If it is a subject, choose *who* or *whoever*. If it is an object, choose *whom* or *whomever*.

EXAMPLES:

Give this prize to [whoever gets the right answer.]

Give this prize to [whomever you like.]

NOTE: Also see pp. 36–38 and pp. 138–139.

MAKING CONNECTIONS:
The Compound-Complex Sentence

REMEMBER:

A *simple* sentence = one independent clause

I watched TV.

Jim and I watched TV.

Jim and I watched TV and ate pizza in the living room.

A *compound* sentence = two independent clauses

I watched TV, and Jim practiced karate.

A *complex* sentence = one independent clause + at least one dependent clause

I watched TV while Jim practiced karate.

I watched the football game that was on TV.

A *compound-complex sentence* = at least two independent clauses + at least one dependent clause

After we finished eating, I watched TV, and Jim practiced karate.

I watched the football game that was on TV, and Jim practiced karate.

MAKE THE RIGHT CONNECTIONS:
Avoid Fragments and Run-ons

We don't always talk in complete sentences, especially when we are asking and answering questions:

"Two packs of gum, please."

"Anything else?"

"Yes, some mints."

"What flavor?"

However, you should always use complete sentences in your writing—unless you're writing a story with conversation in it or quoting someone's exact words. Avoid these common pitfalls:

* Don't write a fragment of a sentence as if it were complete. REMEMBER: Some ideas are incomplete—no matter how long and complicated they may look. Don't let phrases and dependent clauses "hang loose" in your writing. Make sure they are connected to main clauses.

EXAMPLES:

Don't write: She walked across the balance beam. Holding her breath.

(*Holding her breath* is not a sentence. It does not have a subject and a predicate. It cannot stand alone. Since it describes *She,* it can be connected to the sentence that comes before.)

Write: Holding her breath, she walked across the balance beam.

Don't write: I like Mexican food. As long as it's not too hot.

(The second group of words is not a sentence. It has a subject and a predicate, BUT it begins with the words *as long as.* The words *as long as* show that this group of words needs to be connected to a main clause for its meaning to be clear.)

Write: I like Mexican food, as long as it's not too hot.

* Don't connect two complete sentences with just a comma. There are all kinds of *correct*

ways to combine two thoughts in one sentence (see "Writing Tips" in this chapter). A few examples follow.

EXAMPLES:

Don't write: It's still raining, we may have to cancel the track meet.

Use a semicolon:
It's still raining; we may have to cancel the track meet.

Use a comma + a coordinating conjunction:
It's still raining, and we may have to cancel the track meet.

Use a semicolon + a coordinating adverb:
It's still raining; therefore, we may have to cancel the track meet.

Use a subordinating conjunction:
We may have to cancel the track meet, since it's still raining.

NOTE: SOMETIMES IT'S BEST TO JUST WRITE TWO SENTENCES:

It's still raining. We may have to cancel the track meet.

USE IT RIGHT!
A Glossary of Confusing Words

a/an

Use *a* before words that start with a consonant sound.

Use *an* before words that start with a vowel sound.

EXAMPLES:

a basketball, a yo-yo, a universe
(the *u* has a *yoo* sound)

a European country
(the *eur* sounds like *your*)

an apple, an engine, an upside down cake

an honor (the *h* is not pronounced), a habit

able to/able to be

Say: I was able to finish my homework.

Don't say: My homework was able to be finished.

accept/except

Accept means *to take* or *to receive*.

Except means *but*.

EXAMPLES:

Everyone *except* Mimi was there to *accept* the award.

affect/effect

Affect is usually a verb meaning *to have an influence on.*

Effect is usually a noun meaning the *result*.
(Memory tip: effect—result)

EXAMPLES:

The news *affected* her badly.

The news had a bad *effect*.

already/all ready

Already means *previously* or *by this time*.

All ready means all set, all prepared.

EXAMPLE:

The car has *already* been packed. We're *all ready* to go.

altogether/all together

All together means *gathered together in a group*. (the meaning you probably use more often).

Altogether means *entirely*.

EXAMPLES:

We drove to the game *all together* in Jeff's car.

It was *altogether* too crowded.

anywhere/anywheres

The correct word is *anywhere*. DO NOT put an *s* at the end.

all right/alright

Alright is NOT A WORD.

It's ALWAYS ALL RIGHT to use *all right*.

amount/number

Amount tells *how much*. It usually refers to a singular noun.

Number tells *how many*. It refers to a plural noun consisting of items that can be counted.

EXAMPLES:

I used a large *amount* of flour.

The *number* of people at the game amazed us.

bad/badly

See p. 111.

beside/besides

Beside means *next to*. It is always a preposition.

Besides means *in addition to*. It can be a preposition or a coordinating adverb.

EXAMPLES:

Who, *besides* you, would sit *beside* me while I study?

I like working at Pizza Heaven; *besides*, I need the money.

bring/take

Use *bring* when you mean to *come here* with something.

Use *take* when you mean *to go there* with something.

EXAMPLES:

Bring me an apple.

Take these extra chairs to the gym.

can/may

Can means to be able.

May means to have permission. It is also an auxiliary verb expressing possibility.

EXAMPLES:

I *may* go to Florida if I *can* get an airline reservation.

May I be excused?

can't hardly

Can't hardly is a double negative. It should not be used. For more information, see p. 107.

could of

Don't use *of* as an auxiliary verb after could, should, would, might, etc. Say *could have, would have, should have*. For more information, see p. 65.

criteria/criterion

Criterion is the singular form. *Criteria* is the plural.

His decision is based on one *criterion*.

His decision is based on two *criteria*.

done/did

Don't say: He done all the work.

Say: He *did* all the work.

He *has done* all the work.

don't/doesn't

Don't say: It don't work. He don't care.

Say: It *doesn't* work.

He *doesn't* care.

DOUBLE NEGATIVES

Don't use two negative words in close relationship to each other. For more information see p. 107.

etc.

The Latin abbreviation *etc.* is short for *and other things*. Do not use the word *and* before it or you will be saying "and and other things." Do not write etc., etc. or you will be writing "and other things and other things."

farther/further

Farther is used to express physical distances.

Further is used in all other cases.

EXAMPLES:

We traveled *farther* than that last summer.

Ms. Williamson *further* explained the assignment.

fewer/less

Use *fewer* with a plural noun—when the individual items you are talking about can be counted. Use *less* with a singular noun.

EXAMPLES:

Give the child *less soup* than you give the adults.

Give the child *fewer pieces* of candy than he asks for.

good/well

See pp. 110–111.

had of

Don't use these two words together. See pp. 65–66.

had ought/hadn't ought

Never use the auxiliary have or had with *ought*.

EXAMPLES:

Don't say: She had ought to go.

Say: She ought to go. (present)

She ought to have gone. (past)

She ought not to go. (present, negative)

She ought not to have gone. (past negative)

a half/half a/a half a

You can use either *a half* or *half a*. Just remember: one *a* is enough. Never say *a half a*.

EXAMPLES:

Don't say: I had a half an hour to do the job.

Say: I had *a half hour* to do the job.

Or: I had *half an hour* to do the job.

hardly

Hardly is considered a negative word. Avoid using it with other negative words. See p. 107.

imply/infer

The person who is writing or speaking *implies* something.

The person who is reading or listening *infers* something from what he or she reads or hears.

EXAMPLES:

Mother *implied* that I should help out more.

I *inferred* that I was in trouble.

in/into

In is usually used just to express location, not movement.

Into is used to express movement from one place to another.

EXAMPLES:

Grandmother is *in* the living room.

I walked *into* the living room.

its/it's

Its shows possession. *It's* means *it is*. For more information, see p. 33.

kind of a

Don't use the word *a* after *kind of*.

EXAMPLES:

Don't say:　　That *kind of a* car is hard to drive.

　Say:　　That *kind of* car is hard to drive.

learn/teach

A person who gives instruction *teaches*.

A person who receives the instruction *learns*.

153

EXAMPLES:

He *taught* me to play the guitar.

I *learned* fast.

let/leave

Let means *to allow* or to *give permission*.

Leave means *to go away*.

NOTE: You can use either word with *alone*.

You can say: *Let* me alone.

      Or: *Leave* me alone.

In most other cases that might confuse you, the correct choice is usually *let*.

   Let her be.

   Let go of the wire!

   Let it stay there for a while.

lie/lay

Lie means *to rest* or *to recline*. *Lay* means *to put or place* (something). For more help, see pp. 71–72.

like/as/as if

Like is a preposition. It can be followed by a noun or pronoun + modifiers.

EXAMPLES:

You look *like* Leif Garrett.

He seems *like* a good choice for class president.

As and *as if* are conjunctions used to introduce a clause. They are followed by a subject + a verb. Do not use *like* before a subject + a verb.

EXAMPLES:

Don't say: You look *like* you've had a rough day.

     Say: You look *as if* you've had a rough day.

NOTE: *Like* never comes before a subject + a verb. However, it can sometimes be used when a verb is *understood*, as long as the verb is not expressed.

EXAMPLES:

She dances *like* a professional ballerina.

loan/lend

Loan is a noun. *Lend* is a verb.

EXAMPLES:

I took out a *loan* at the bank. They *lent* me $500.

Lend me a pencil, will you?

medium/media

Medium is singular. *Media* is plural.

EXAMPLE:

Television is a powerful *medium*.

All of the mass *media* are powerful.

might of/must of

Never use *of* as an auxiliary verb. Say *might have*, *must have*, or the contractions *might've* and *must've*.

most/almost/mostly

Most means *the greatest number, the greatest amount,* or *to the greatest degree.*

Almost means *nearly.*

Mostly means *mainly* or *almost entirely.*

EXAMPLES:

Most of us are *almost* ready to start.

The people *most* in need of help are the ones who have lost their homes.

I am worried *mostly* about them.

nowhere/nowheres

Nowhere is the correct form. Do not put an *s* at the end of it.

off/from

Don't use the word *off* for the word *from*.

EXAMPLES:

Don't say: I borrowed this jacket *off* Tony.

Say: I borrowed this jacket *from* Tony.

ought

See *had ought*.

raise/rise

Raise means *to move something upward*. *Rise* means *to go upward*. For more help, see pp. 73–74.

real/really

Real is an adjective. *Really* is an adverb. For more help, see pp. 110–111.

sit/set

Sit means *to take a seat* or *to be situated*. *Set* means *to put* or *to place something*. For more help, see pp. 74–75.

sure/surely

Sure is an adjective. *Surely* is an adverb. For more information, see pp. 110–111.

than/then

Than is a conjunction used in making comparisons. *Then* tells when.

EXAMPLES:

Then Steve walked into the room.

He is taller *than* I am.

them/they/those

Don't say: *Them* are the ones I want.
For more information, see p. 40.

there/their/they're
See p. 33.

this here/that there
See p. 40.

this kind/these kinds
The word *kind* is singular, even when it is followed by plural nouns. Always use singular modifiers and a singular verb with it.

EXAMPLE:

This kind of mittens *is* hard to find.

The word *kinds* is plural. It takes plural modifiers and a plural verb.

EXAMPLE:

These two *kinds* of ice cream *are* different.

to/two/too
Two is the number.

To means *toward*.

Too means *also* or *excessively*.

EXAMPLES:

I want to go *too*. That is *too* much.

That will be *two* dollars.

Let's walk *to* the store.

try and/try to
Try to is correct.

EXAMPLES:

Don't say: I will *try and* help you.

Say: I will *try to* help you.

CAPITALIZATION POINTERS

CAPITALIZE PROPER NOUNS—THE NAMES OF SPECIFIC PERSONS, PLACES, AND THINGS:

* Capitalize the names of the months, the days of the week, and holidays. Do not capitalize the names of the four seasons.

  EXAMPLES:

  Sunday, Thanksgiving, January, summer, spring, winter, fall (autumn)

* Capitalize the names of particular places: states, countries, rivers, oceans, cities, streets, parks, etc.

  EXAMPLES:

  Florida, the United States, the Mississippi River, the Atlantic Ocean, Valley Road

* Capitalize the names of schools, companies, buildings, government departments, and organizations. (Do *not* capitalize such words as *a, an, the,* and *of* except when they are the first word and then only if they are part of the title.)

  EXAMPLES:

  Brookville High School, General Motors, Department of Commerce, the Empire State Building, Boy Scouts of America, *The New York Times*

* Capitalize words that indicate a person's rank or title when they are used *with* the person's name or *in place of* the person's name.

EXAMPLES:

Captain Hook, Dr. Smith

"Thank you for coming, Judge."

"Hurry, Doctor, it's an emergency!"

BUT: a captain, my doctor, the judge

* Capitalize the names of some important titles even when they are not used as names.

EXAMPLES:

the President of the United States, the Prime Minister, the Secretary of Defense

* Capitalize words such as *mother, father, uncle, aunt,* etc., only when they are used as names.

EXAMPLES:

Uncle Bill, Aunt Sarah

My mother's brother is my uncle.

Tell Dad I might be late.

* Capitalize the names of religions, nationalities, and languages—and the adjectives that are made from these names.

EXAMPLES:

Jewish, Christian, Italian-American, English, French

* Capitalize the Deity and the names of sacred documents.

EXAMPLES:

God, the Bible, the Torah

NOTE: Do not capitalize the word *god* when it refers to the gods of mythology.

* Capitalize the names of historic periods and events.

EXAMPLES:

the Civil War, the Middle Ages

* Capitalize brand names of products. Do not capitalize the nouns that follow a brand name unless they are part of the name.

EXAMPLES:

Bird's Eye vegetables, a Chevrolet car

* Capitalize the names of planets and other heavenly bodies. Do not capitalize *sun* or *moon*. Do not capitalize *earth* unless it is used with the names of other planets.

EXAMPLES:

Mars is one of the closest planets to Earth.

The sun and moon revolve around the earth.

* Capitalize *east, west, north,* and *south* ONLY when they refer to a particular section of the country or the world.

EXAMPLES:

Turn south on Route 3.

Business is booming in the South.

She had a Southern accent.

They visited the Far East.

* Capitalize all words in a title except for *a, an, the,* short prepositions, and short conjunctions (unless they are the first or last word).

EXAMPLES:

Romeo and Juliet, The Scarlet Letter,

"The Secret Life of Walter Mitty"

Mutiny on the Bounty

CAPITALIZE PROPER ADJECTIVES— ADJECTIVES MADE FROM PROPER NOUNS.

EXAMPLES:

Chinese food, American economy

CAPITALIZE THE FIRST WORD:

* in a sentence:
  She asked my opinion.

* in a quotation whether the quotation is a complete sentence or not:
  I said, "Why don't we start practicing tomorrow?"
  He said, "Not today?"

* in the greeting and closing of a letter:
  Dear Terry, Yours truly,

DO NOT CAPITALIZE:

* school subjects UNLESS they are derived from proper nouns or refer to a particular course name.
  EXAMPLES:
  English, Spanish, American history
  (derived from proper nouns)
  history, biology, math
  Biology II, Introduction to Calculus

* the names of animals, plants, diseases, games, foods, and musical instruments UNLESS they contain a proper adjective.
  EXAMPLES:
  collie, French poodle, trumpet, French horn, chicken pox, German measles, oak, California redwood

PUNCTUATION POINTERS

THE PERIOD

* Use a period at the end of any sentence that does not ask a question or express strong feelings.

EXAMPLE:

I have a new bike.

* Use a period after initials and most abbreviations.

EXAMPLES:

Mr. J. G. Henderson

Helen Demare, Ph.D.

etc., *e.g.*, B.C.

U.S.A., tsp.

THE QUESTION MARK

* Use a question mark at the end of a question.

EXAMPLE:

What happened to my science project?

THE EXCLAMATION MARK

* Use an exclamation mark after an expression of strong feeling.

EXAMPLES:

Let's get out of here fast!

Help! The monster has come to life!

THE COMMA

* Use commas to separate words, phrases, and clauses in a series.

EXAMPLES:

Carol, Sandy, and I went together.

I rolled up the car windows, took down the laundry, and closed the storm windows.

I want to know when we're going, who's taking us, and what I should wear.

* Use commas to separate two or more adjectives of equal importance.

TEST: If you can change the order of the adjectives or put *and* between them, use a comma. DO NOT put a comma between the last adjective and the noun.

EXAMPLE:

I planted the flowers in a small plastic container.

I rode the gentle, obedient horse.

* Use commas to set off adjectives that come after a noun.

EXAMPLES:

My horse, gentle and obedient, was easy to ride.

* Use a comma before *and, but, or, nor, for, so,* and *yet* when they connect two independent clauses. (If the clauses are very short, you may not need a comma.)

EXAMPLES:

We asked Mr. Jacoby to help, and he agreed to meet with us.

We asked him to help and he did.

NOTE: DO NOT use a comma before these conjunctions when they join the two parts of a compound verb. For more help, see p. 129.

EXAMPLE:

We *asked* Mr. Jacoby for help and *offered* to meet with him sometime after school.

* Use a comma after certain kinds of words, phrases, and clauses—*when they begin a sentence:*

  * after words such as *yes, no, oh,* and *well*

    EXAMPLES:

    Yes, I think I will stay for band practice.

    Well, let's start from the begnning.

  * after adverb clauses that begin a sentence

    EXAMPLE:

    After this show is over, let's turn off the TV.

  * after a participial phrase that begins a sentence

    EXAMPLE:

    Poking around in the refrigerator, I finally found what I was looking for.

  * after long prepositional phrases that begin a sentence

    EXAMPLE:

    During the blizzard last winter, we couldn't go outside.

    NOTE: If the prepositional phrase is short, you don't really need a comma.

    EXAMPLE:

    In 1776 the Declaration of Independence was signed.

* Use a comma to set off a noun of direct address.

EXAMPLE:

Jane, will you help me?

Will you help me, Jane?

* Use commas to set off interrupters such as *you see*, *I believe*, *by the way*, *for example*, etc.

EXAMPLES:

His name, by the way, is John.

Judy, for example, won't be able to get here on time.

* Use commas to set off any extra word, phrase, or clause that is not ESSENTIAL to the meaning of the sentence. This important use of the comma is explained on p. 140.

* Use commas to show that two parts of a sentence are being contrasted.

EXAMPLE:

He plays the guitar, not the drums.

* Use a comma to avoid confusion.

EXAMPLE:

A few minutes before, the game had started.

* Use commas between the parts of a date, except between the month and the day.

EXAMPLE:

Saturday, July 11, 1981

NOTE: When the date occurs in the middle of a sentence, add a comma after the year.

EXAMPLE:

On Saturday, July 11, 1981, we will celebrate his birthday.

* Use commas between the parts of an address.

165

EXAMPLE:

925 Sunset Drive, Anderson, New Jersey

NOTE: When the address occurs in the middle of a sentence, add a comma after the last word in the address.

EXAMPLE:

Should I write 925 Sunset Drive, Anderson, New Jersey, on the envelope?

THE SEMICOLON

* Use a semicolon between main clauses that are not joined by *and, or, for, but, so,* or *yet.*

EXAMPLE:

I wanted to take the bus; John didn't.

* When two main clauses are joined by words such as *however, also, besides, indeed, otherwise, nonetheless, then,* and *thus,* use a semicolon BEFORE the connecting word and a COMMA after.

EXAMPLE:

I know this sounds incredible; however, it is a true story.

NOTE: For more information, see p. 128.

* In a sentence that has many commas, a semicolon may be necessary to separate main clauses or items in a series.

EXAMPLES:

I bought a new skirt, which was on sale at Lyndon's; a pair of jeans, which are a perfect color and fit really well; and three new blouses.

My sturdy, reliable bike, a three-speed that I've had since the third grade, finally needs to be replaced; and I hope I can get a ten-speed now.

THE COLON

* Use a colon to introduce a list of items, especially after the words *follows* and *the following*.

EXAMPLE:

The following people have been chosen to represent our class: John, Rebecca, Marianne, and Tim.

* Use a colon after the greeting in a business letter.
Dear Madam: Dear Sir:

THE DASH

* Use a dash to indicate a sudden break in the flow of a sentence or to set off an idea in a dramatic way.

EXAMPLE:

She asked me to call her—I can't imagine why—at ten o'clock.

THE HYPHEN

* Use a hyphen to write out numbers and to make a compound adjective out of two or more words.

EXAMPLES:

three-hundred-seventeen

a six-dollar seat

the Warrior-Eagle game

a well-known skater

* Use a hyphen to divide a word at the end of a line. Always divide between the syllables. Check a good dictionary when you are not sure how to divide a word.

* Use a hyphen after certain prefixes, such as *ex-* and *self-*.

EXAMPLES:

self-confidence   an ex-boxer

THE APOSTROPHE

* Use an apostrophe to show possession in nouns. For rules on how to make nouns possessive, see pp. 23–26.

* Use an apostrophe to indicate missing letters in a contraction.

EXAMPLES:

don't, wouldn't, wasn't, would've

QUOTATION MARKS

* Use quotation marks around the titles of short works such as magazine articles, short stories, short poems, essays, and chapter titles.

EXAMPLES:

"The Lady or the Tiger" is one of my favorite stories.

Chapter 7 is entitled "Making Connections."

* Use quotation marks to indicate someone's exact words.

EXAMPLE:

She said, "I still have a chance to pass this course."

BUT: She said that she still had a chance to pass this course.

NOTE: Always place periods and commas *inside* the quotation marks.

EXAMPLES:

"Don't forget," he said, "your favorite show is on tonight."

NOTE: Always place colons and semicolons *outside* the quotation marks.

EXAMPLE:

She said, "Wait until Friday"; however, Friday will be too late.

NOTE: Put a question mark *inside* the quotation marks when the quotation itself is a question.

EXAMPLE:

She asked, "Do you believe in Santa Claus?"

NOTE: Place a question mark *outside* the quotation marks when the whole sentence is a question.

EXAMPLE:

Did you hear me say, "Come in and have a seat"?

NOTE: The same rule applies to exclamation marks.

EXAMPLES:

"Get out of here!" she screamed.

Don't you dare say, "Do it yourself"!

Use single quotation marks to indicate a quotation within a quotation.

EXAMPLE:

She said, "Have you read Maureen Daly's story 'Sixteen'?"

"The label did say, 'Open carefully,' " she reminded me.

ITALICS (Underlining)

Italics is a kind of type that slants. *This sentence is printed in italics.* When you are writing or typing, indicate italics by *underlining*.

* Use italics (underlining) to indicate titles of books, movies, plays, magazines, and newspapers.

EXAMPLES:

Bananas, Seventeenth Summer, Grease,
The New York Times

* Use italics (underlining) to show that you are talking about words and letters as such.

EXAMPLE:

Does that word end with *d* or *t*?
I always forget how to spell *receive*.

INDEX